Balance Math™ & More!

Level 2

Balance Math™ & More! Series

Level 1 Level 2 Level 3

Balance Math™ Teaches Algebra

Written by

Robert Femiano

Graphic Design by

Scott Slyter

Cover Design by

Annette Langenstein

THE CRITICAL THINKING CO.™
www.CriticalThinking.com
Phone: 800-458-4849 • Fax: 831-393-3277
P.O. Box 1610 • Seaside • CA 93955-1610
ISBN 978-1-60144-277-2

Printed in the United States of America by McNaughton & Gunn, Inc., Saline, MI (Jan. 2013)

TABLE OF CONTENTS

Introduction.....ii
Balance Math™ 1, 2, 4, 6, 7, 10, 12, 13, 15, 17, 18, 21, 23, 25, 27, 30, 32, 35, 36, 39
Inside-Out Math..... 3, 8, 11, 14, 19, 22, 26, 28, 31, 34, 37
Tic Tac Math 5, 9, 16, 20, 24, 29, 33, 38
Hints 40
Answers.....41

The Value of *Balance Math™ and More!*

These activities sharpen students' critical thinking and computational skills while developing their algebraic reasoning. The first book in the series (Level 1) focuses on addition and subtraction of whole numbers. The second book (Level 2) focuses on multiplication and division of whole numbers and a few fractions. The third book (Level 3) involves addition, subtraction, division, and multiplication of whole numbers, fractions, and decimals. The increasing difficulty level within each book is designed to scaffold students' conceptual understanding of the targeted operations from beginning to advanced achievement. Try one of these intriguing puzzles — and then try to stop!

Teaching Suggestions

Balance Math™ and More! activities are unique because their solutions require mathematical reasoning, critical thinking, and computational skills, making them fun, but challenging. Teachers should review the directions with students on all three types of puzzles (Inside-Out Math, Tic Tac Math, and Balance Math™) and cooperatively work through some of them with students until they can demonstrate how to correctly solve the problems independently. If students become stumped, first encourage perseverance and patience by reminding them that people do puzzles because they enjoy being puzzled. Like all puzzlers, students may occasionally need a hint. For Inside-Out Math or Tic Tac Math puzzles, use the answer pages to provide them with the correct number needed next. You can jumpstart their thinking for Balance Math™ puzzles by using the hints provided on page 40.

Balance Math™: Students should examine the balanced scales to deduce and calculate the value of any one shape which can then be substituted on another balance and so on, until the solution is found. These puzzles are also great stepping-stones to showing students the basics of balancing and solving algebraic equations.

Inside-Out Math: Students need to reverse their thinking, using the inverse relationships between addition and subtraction and multiplication with division to solve the puzzles.

Tic Tac Math: Three in a row wins, but can you figure out the correct order to complete all rows, columns, and diagonals?

About the Author

A longtime puzzle fan, Robert Femiano is a Seattle public school elementary educator who has been for most of his 35-year teaching career. For more than a decade of this time, he was also adjunct faculty at Seattle Pacific University, conducting math methods courses. His publications include *Algebraic Problem Solving in the Primary Grades* in the National Council for Teachers of Mathematics peer-reviewed journal and *Balance Benders*™ by The Critical Thinking Co.™. In 2002, he won the highest honor in education, the Presidential Award for Excellence in Mathematics and Science Teaching.

Use the balanced scales to find the missing numbers.

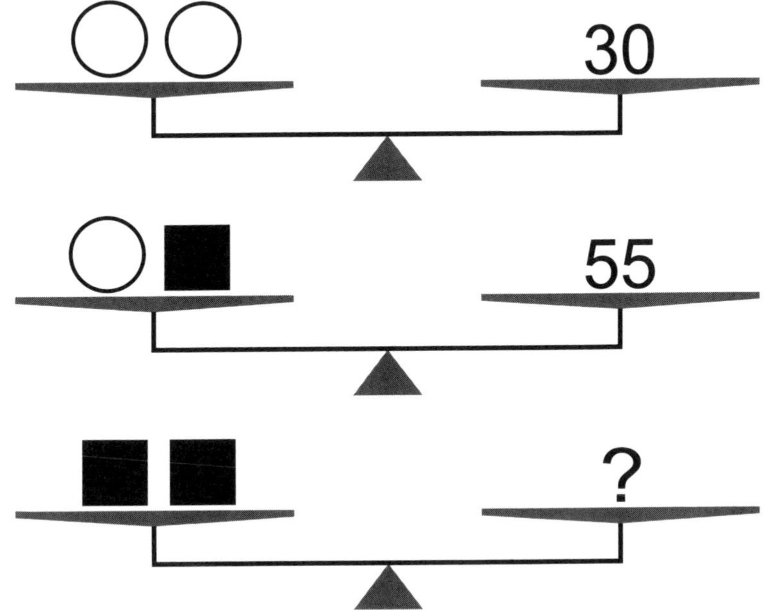

Problem 1

? = ...

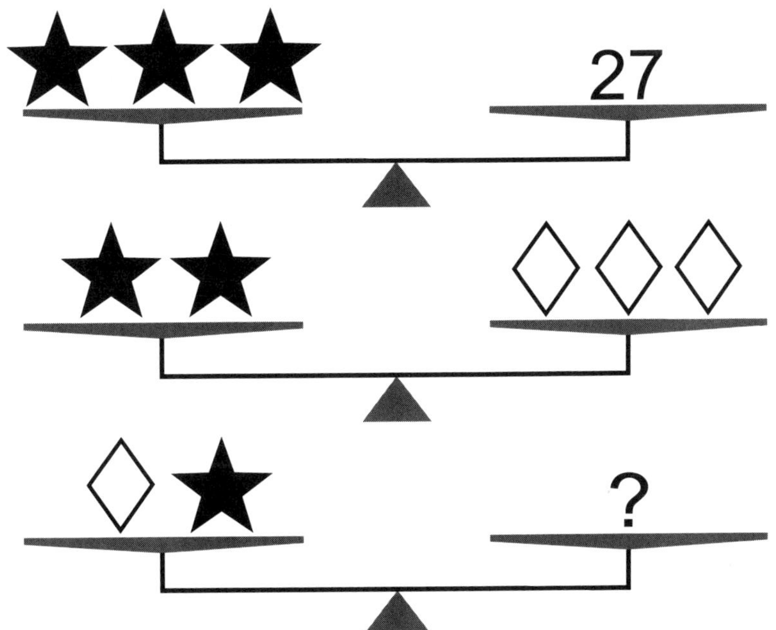

Problem 2

? = ...

Use the balanced scales to find the missing numbers.

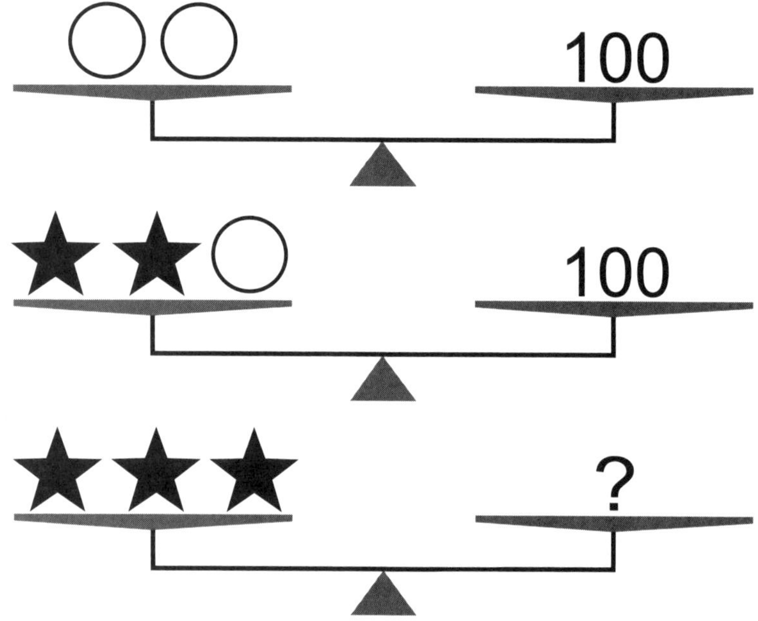

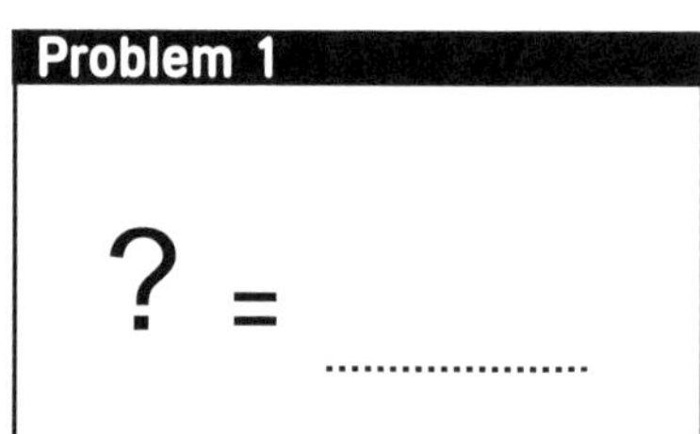

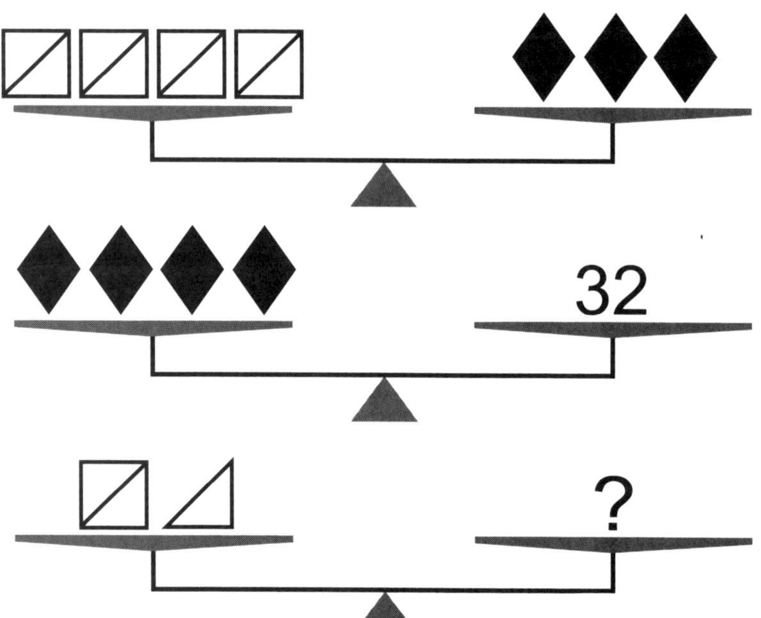

Problem 2

? = ...

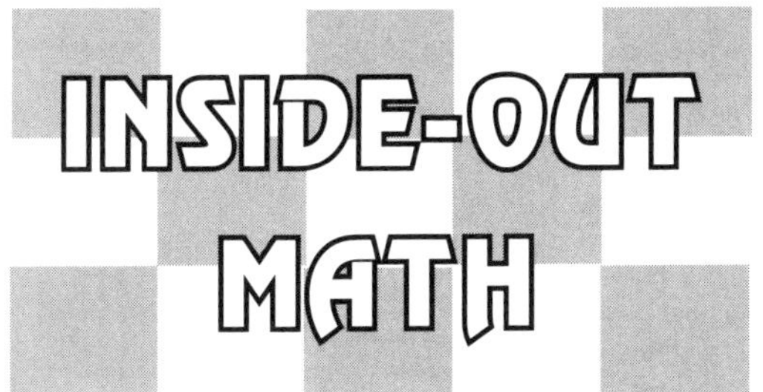

Use the clues to find the missing values.

Problem 1

a: 10	a+c: 50	a+d: ....
b:	b+c: 100	b+d: 80
	c:	d: ....

Problem 2

a:	a+c: 150	a+d: 120
b: 50	b+c: 110	b+d: ....
	c:	d: ....

Problem 3

a:	a+c:	a+d: 110
b:	b+c: 100	b+d: 130
	c: 65	d: ....

Problem 4

a:	a+c: 125	a+d: 75
b:	b+c: 275	b+d: ....
	c:	d: 25

Use the balanced scales to find the missing numbers.

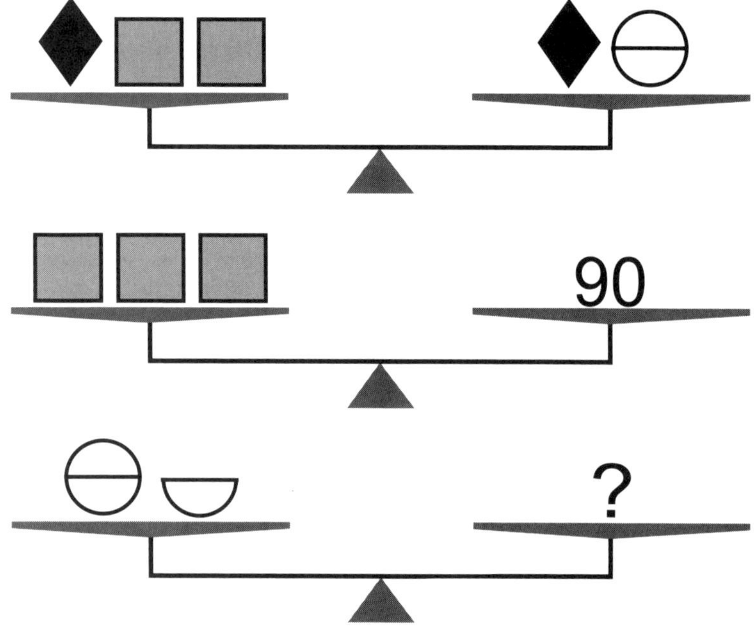

Problem 1

? = ...

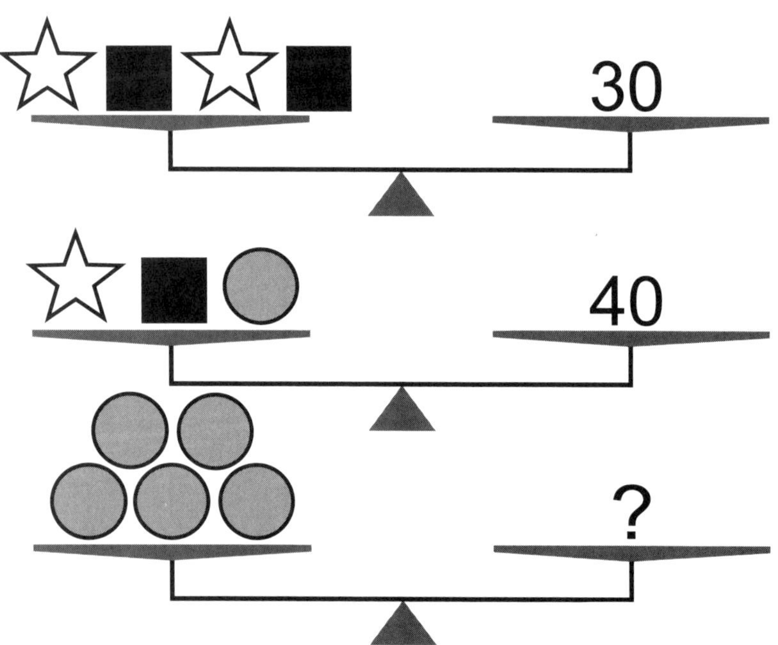

Problem 2

? = ...

All rows, columns, and three numeral diagonals must add up to the same sum. Write the total and then fill in the empty spaces.

Problem 1

		8
2	10	18

Total: ....

Problem 2

		14
	13	
12	11	

Total: ....

Problem 3

10	9	
11		
9		

Total: ....

Problem 4

		40
70		30
		80

Total: ....

Use the balanced scales to find the missing numbers.

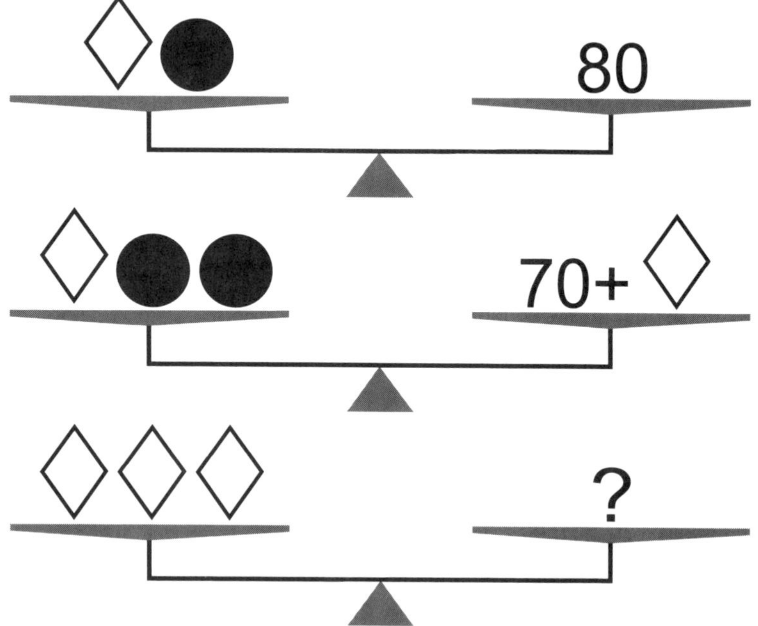

Problem 1

? = ...

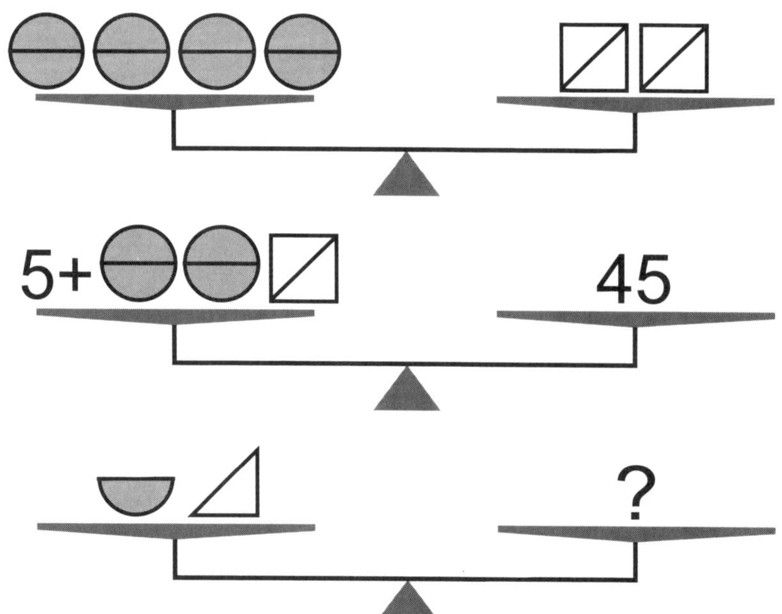

Problem 2

? = ...

Use the balanced scales
to find the missing numbers.

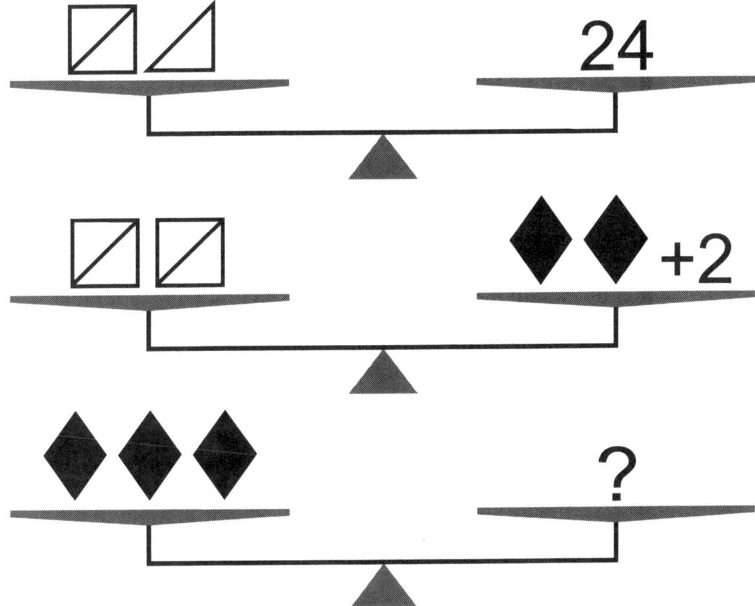

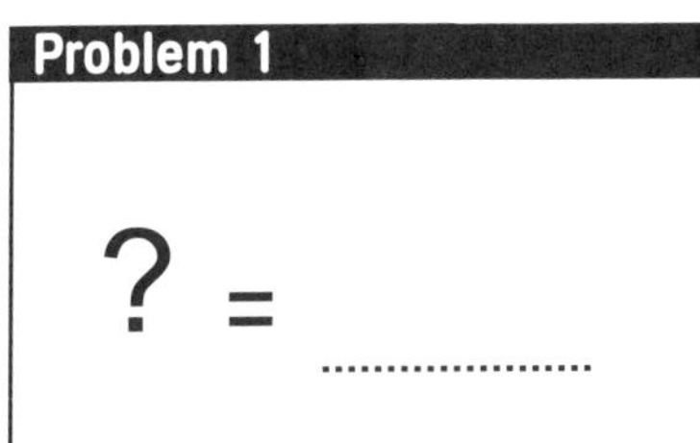

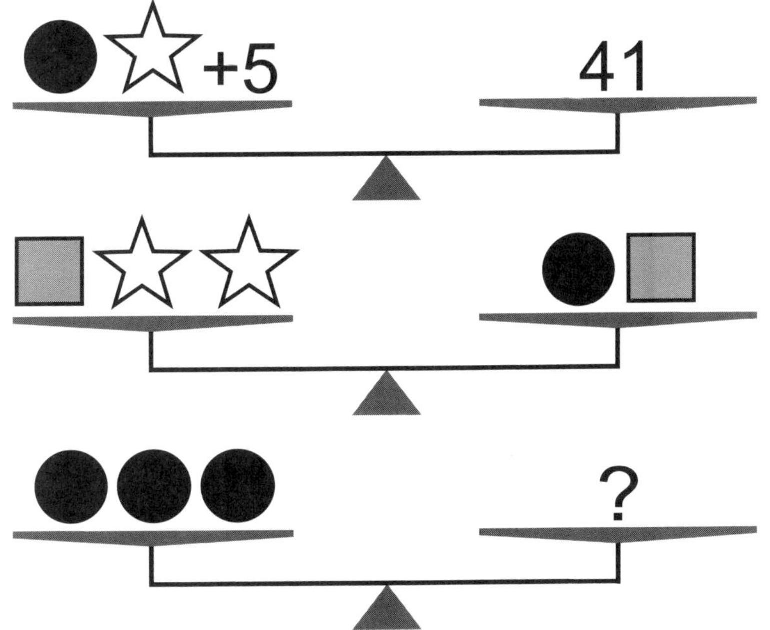

Problem 2

? = ...

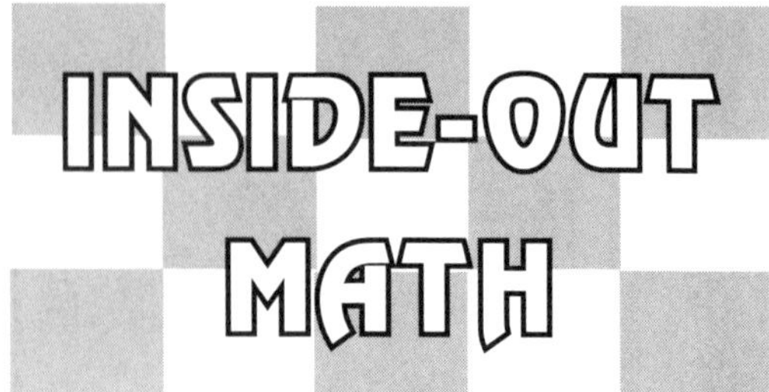

Use the clues to find the missing values.

Problem 1

a: 37
b: ....

a+c	a+d
66	....
b+c	**b+d**
93	101

c: ....
d: ....

Problem 2

a: ....
b: 77

a+c	a+d
145	184
b+c	**b+d**
136	....

c: ....
d: ....

Problem 3

a: ....
b: ....

a+c	a+d
....	403
b+c	**b+d**
393	321

c: 256
d: ....

Problem 4

a: ....
b: ....

a+c	a+d
1,010	1,860
b+c	**b+d**
....	2,100

c: ....
d: 1,730

All rows, columns, and three numeral diagonals must add up to the same sum. Write the total and then fill in the empty spaces.

Problem 1

45		
	55	
	75	65

Total: ....

Problem 2

111		124
136		
122		

Total: ....

Problem 3

	80	
40	120	140

Total: ....

Problem 4

51	9	39
	33	

Total: ....

Use the balanced scales to find the missing numbers.

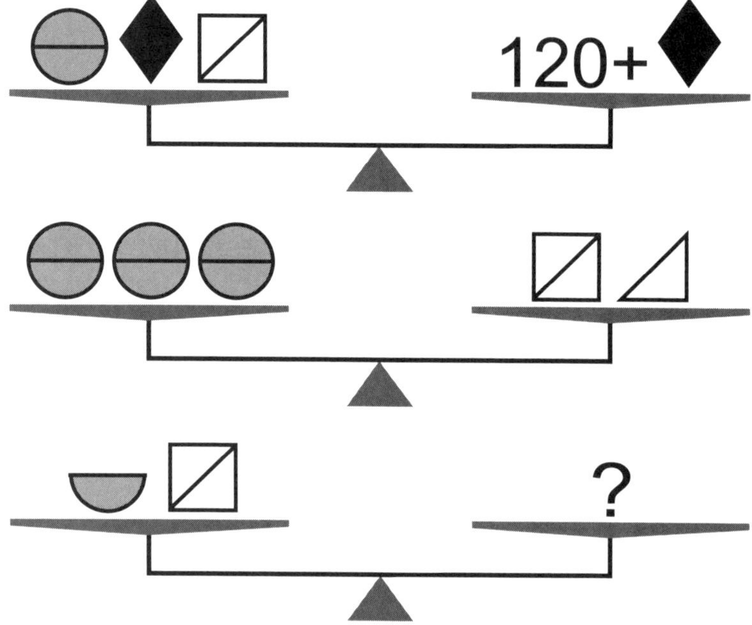

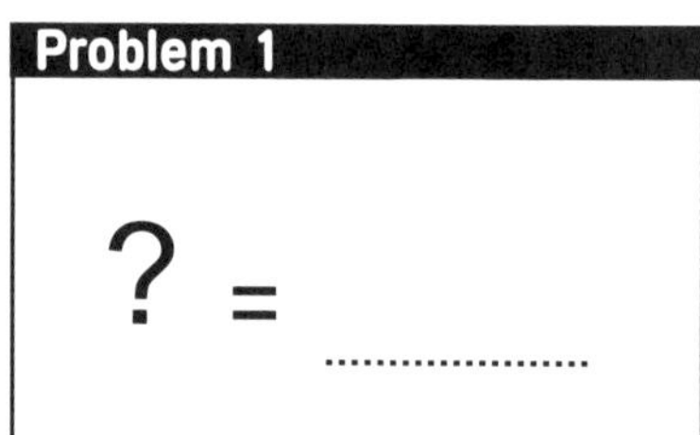

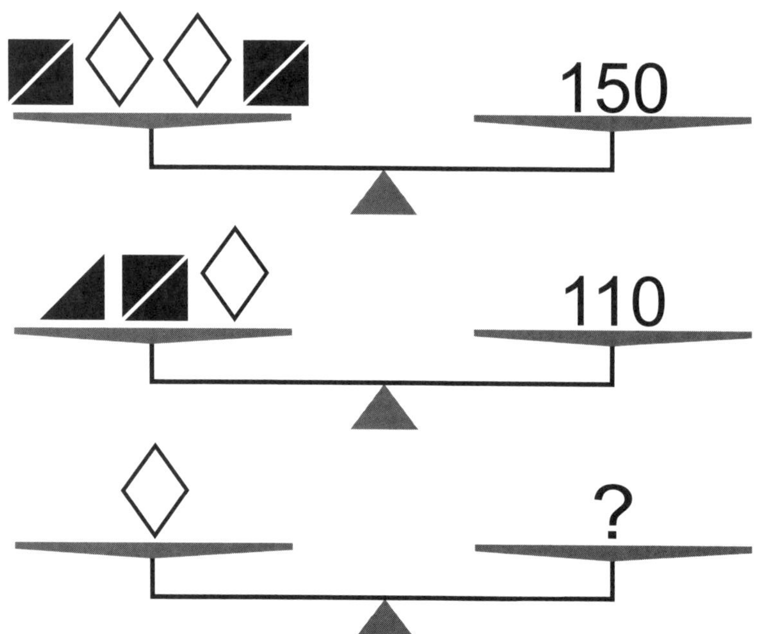

Problem 2

? = ...

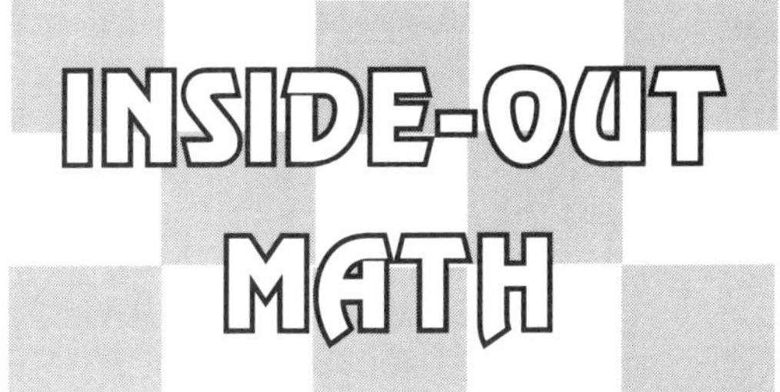

Use the clues to find the missing values.

Problem 1

a 110	a-c 80	a-d ....
b	b-c 50	b-d 30
	c	d ....

Problem 2

a	a-c 590	a-d 370
b 810	b-c 650	b-d ....
	c	d ....

Problem 3

a	a-c	a-d 57
b	b-c 54	b-d 45
	c 27	d ....

Problem 4

a	a-c 86	a-d 66
b	b-c 133	b-d ....
	c	d 101

Use the balanced scales
to find the missing numbers.

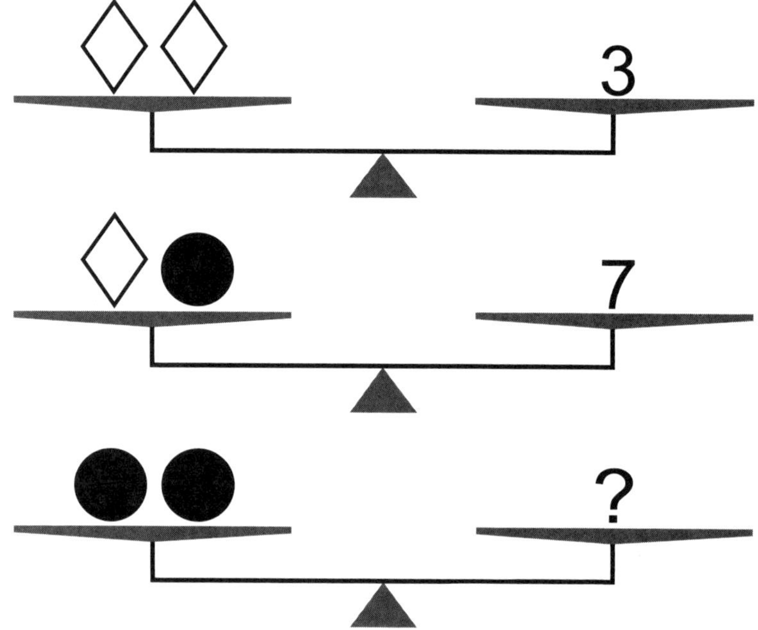

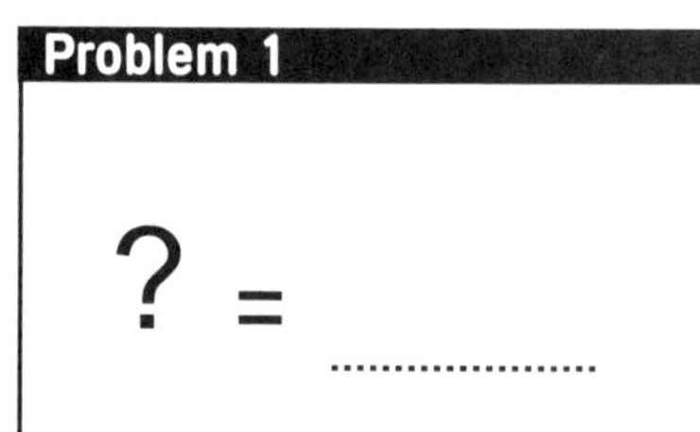

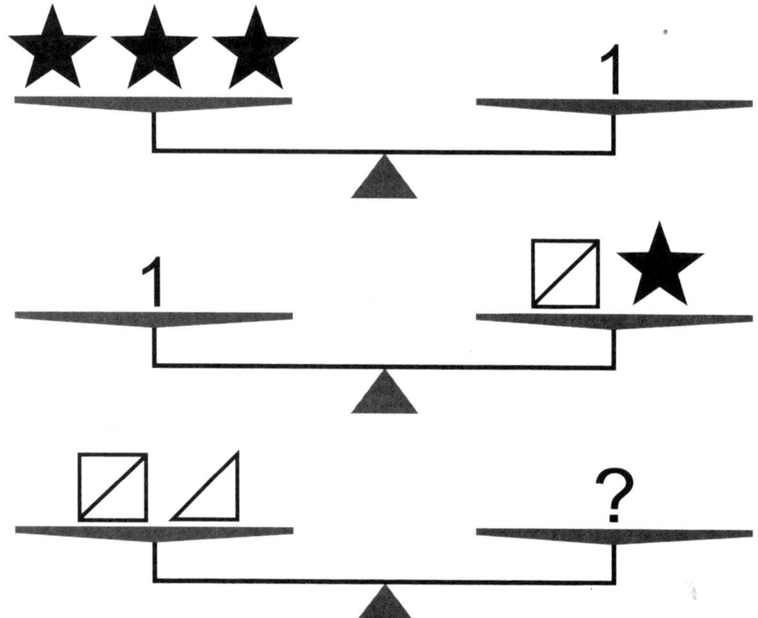

Problem 2

? = ...

Use the balanced scales to find the missing numbers.

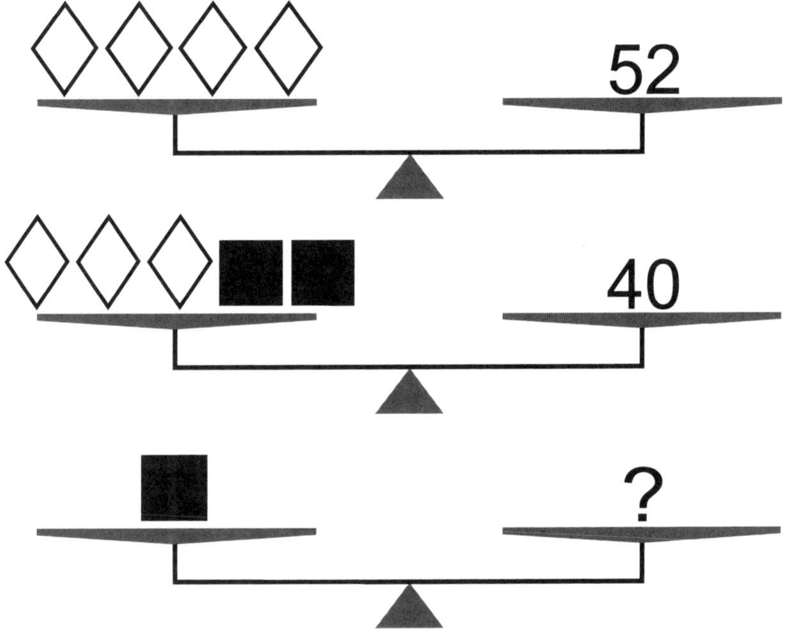

Problem 1

? = ...

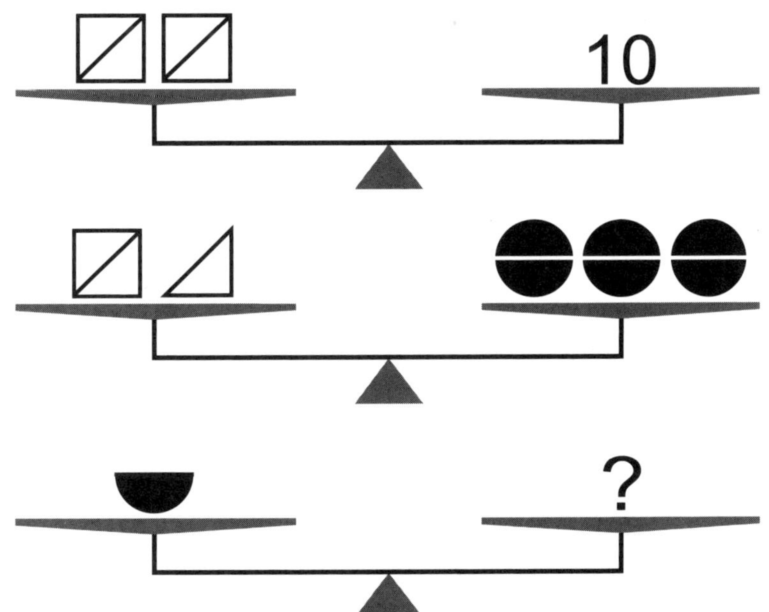

Problem 2

? = ...

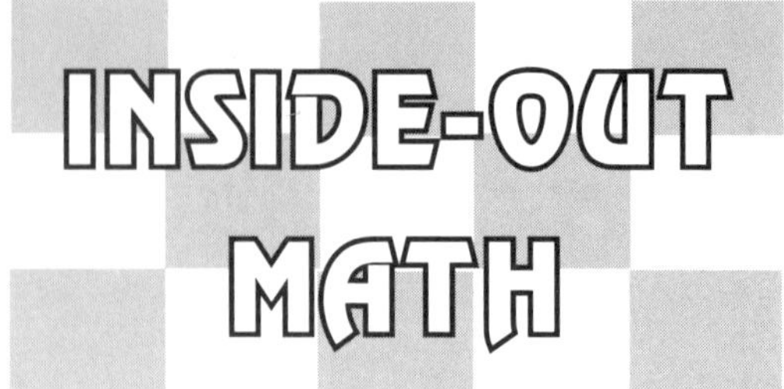

Use the clues to find the missing values.

Problem 1

a 92	a-c 55	a-d ....
b	b-c 47	b-d 29
	c	d ....

Problem 2

a	a-c 39	a-d 47
b 132	b-c 46	b-d ....
	c	d ....

Problem 3

a	a-c	a-d 214
b	b-c 159	b-d 118
	c 148	d ....

Problem 4

a	a-c 7,350	a-d 3,930
b	b-c 7,970	b-d ....
	c	d 4,770

Use the balanced scales to find the missing numbers.

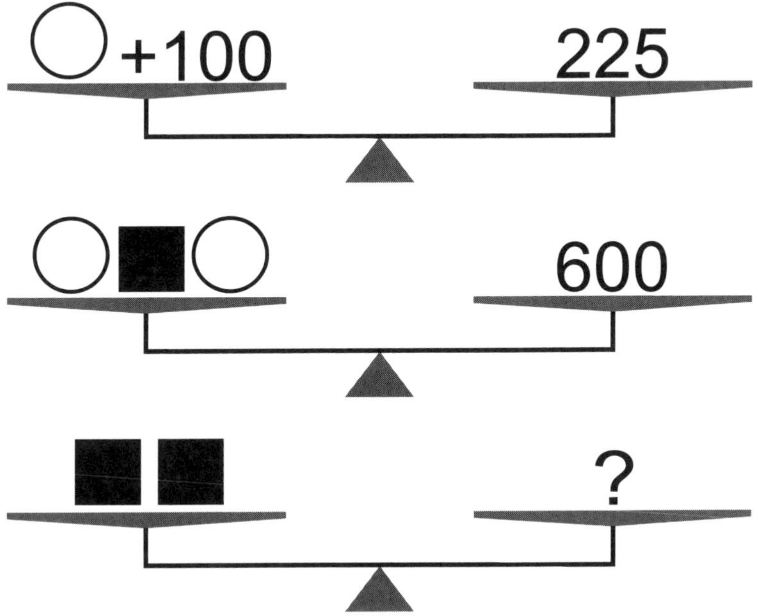

Problem 1

? = ...

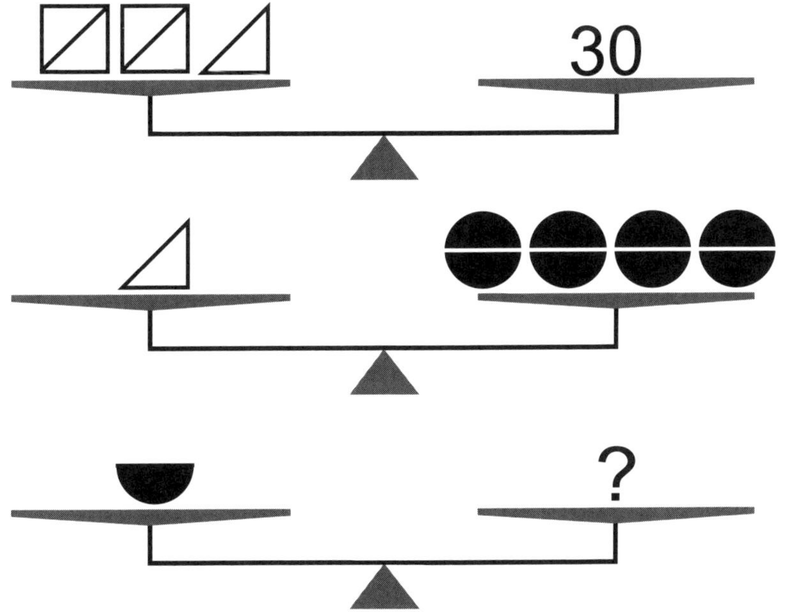

Problem 2

? = ...

All rows, columns, and three numeral diagonals must add up to the same sum. Write the total and then fill in the empty spaces.

Problem 1

480	60	
	300	
	540	

Total: ....

Problem 2

		185
125	95	245

Total: ....

Problem 3

		44
	68	
92		76

Total: ....

Problem 4

109		103
		79
		37

Total: ....

Use the balanced scales
to find the missing numbers.

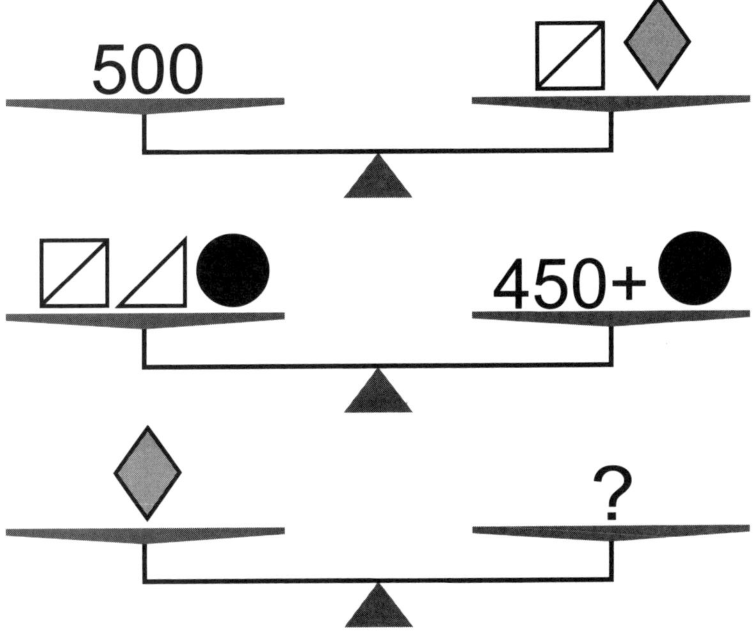

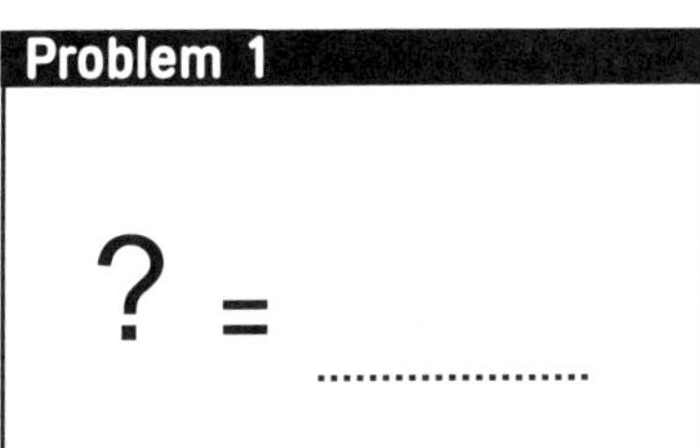

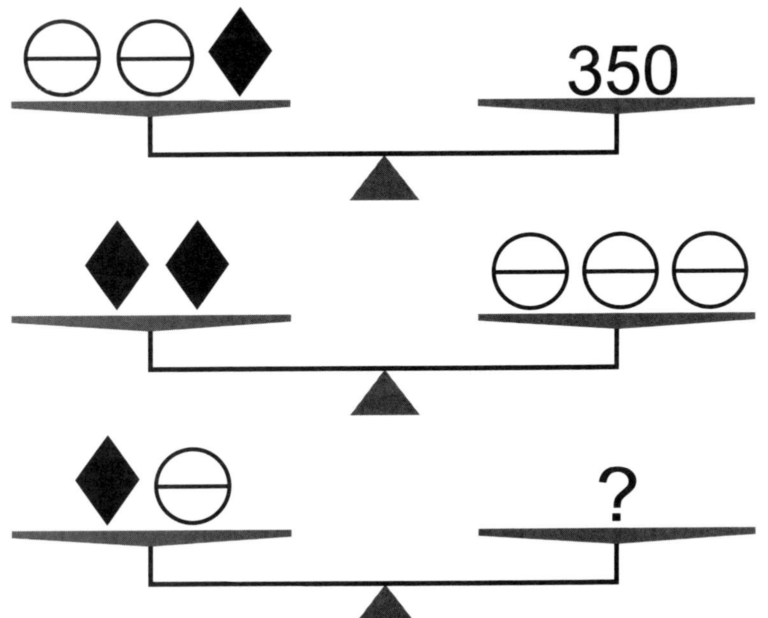

Problem 2

? = ...

Use the balanced scales to find the missing numbers.

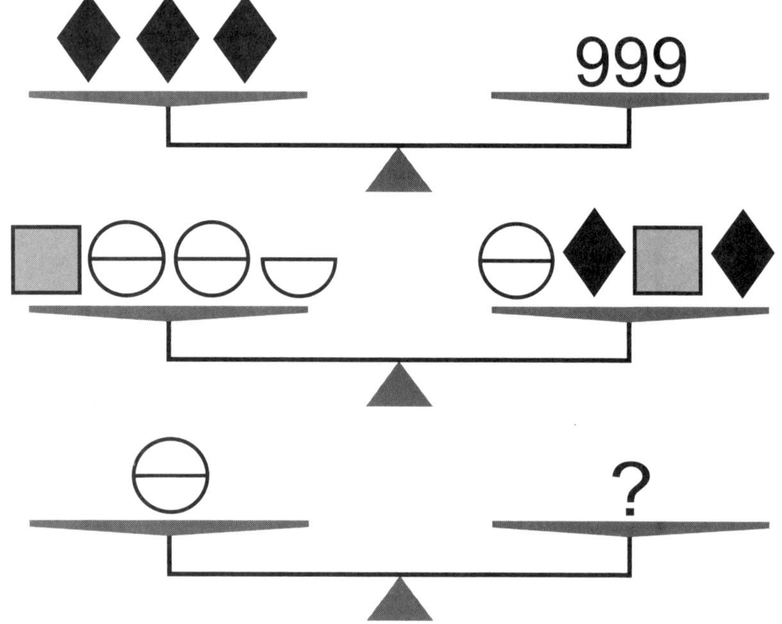

Problem 1

? = ...

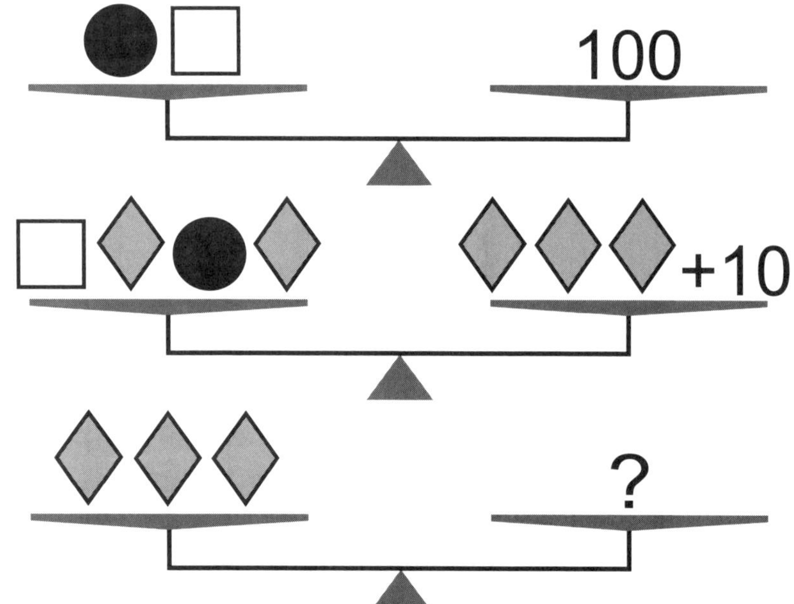

Problem 2

? = ...

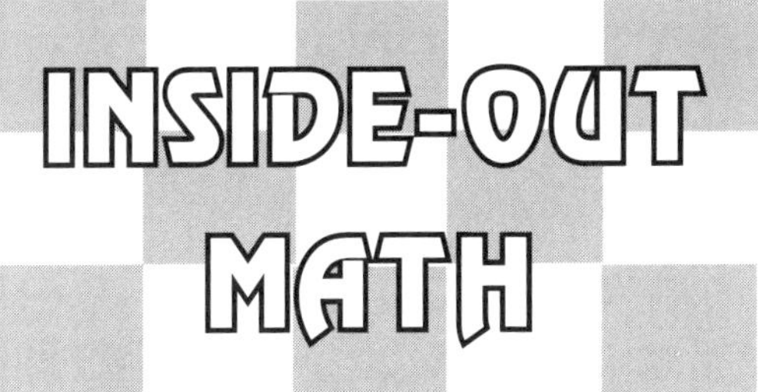

Use the clues to find the missing values.

Problem 1

	c:	d: ....
a: 10,200	a+c:	a+d: 21,100
b:	b+c: 26,700	b+d: 22,800

Problem 2

	c:	d: ....
a:	a+c: 11,111	a+d: 11,101
b: 1,111	b+c: 11,000	b+d: ....

Problem 3

	c: 4,859	d: ....
a:	a+c: 8,610	a+d: 7,729
b:	b+c:	b+d: 9,041

Problem 4

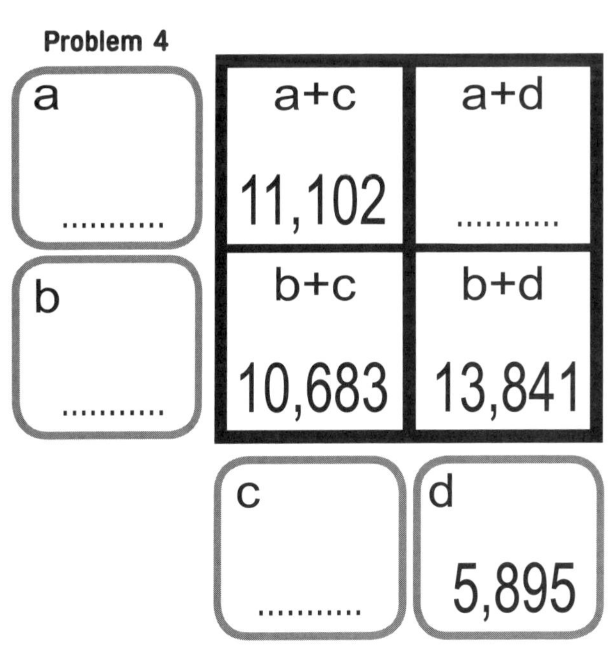

	c:	d: 5,895
a:	a+c: 11,102	a+d: ....
b:	b+c: 10,683	b+d: 13,841

All rows, columns, and three numeral diagonals must add up to the same sum. Write the total and then fill in the empty spaces.

Problem 1

129		
	111	
21		93

Total: ....

Problem 2

	118	
	136	
145	154	

Total: ....

Problem 3

83		
138	149	94

Total: ....

Problem 4

		28
52	148	
268		

Total: ....

Use the balanced scales to find the missing numbers.

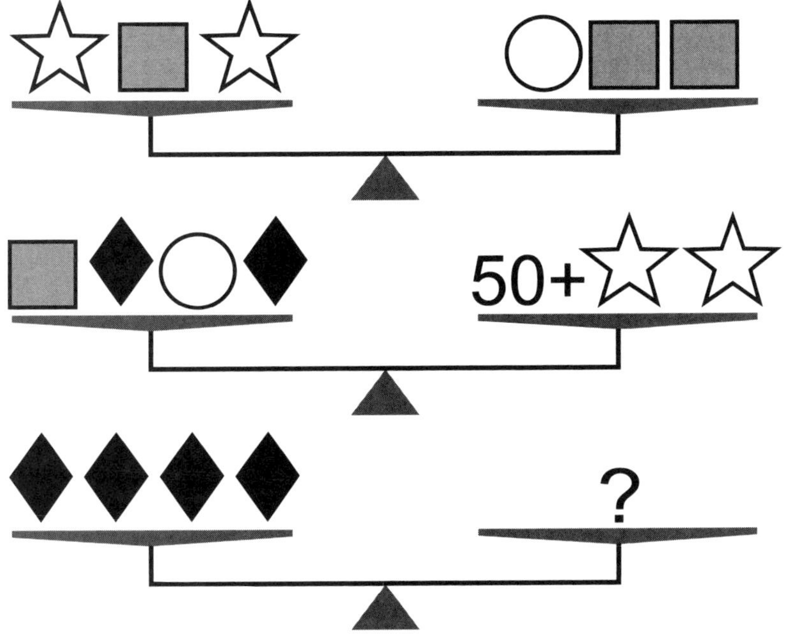

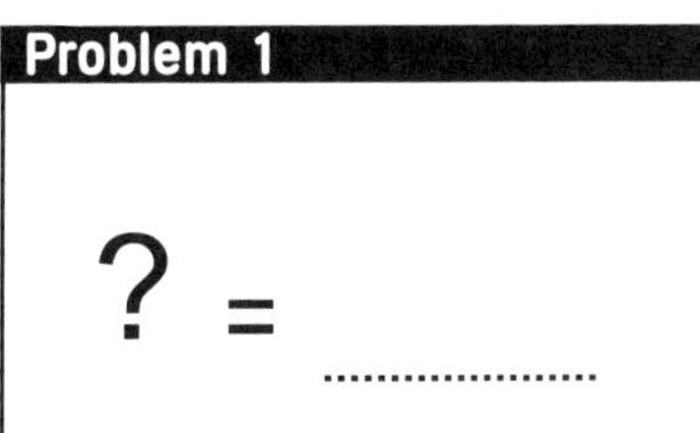

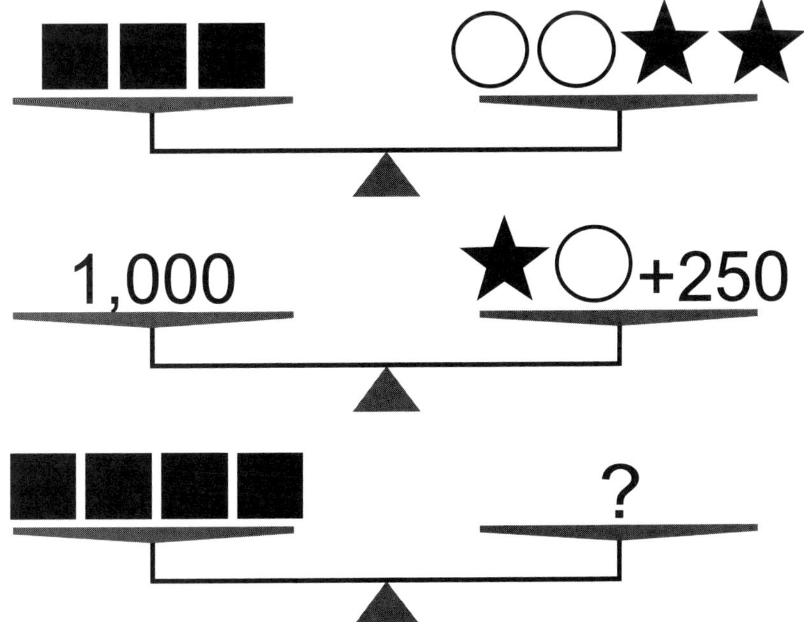

Problem 2

? = ...

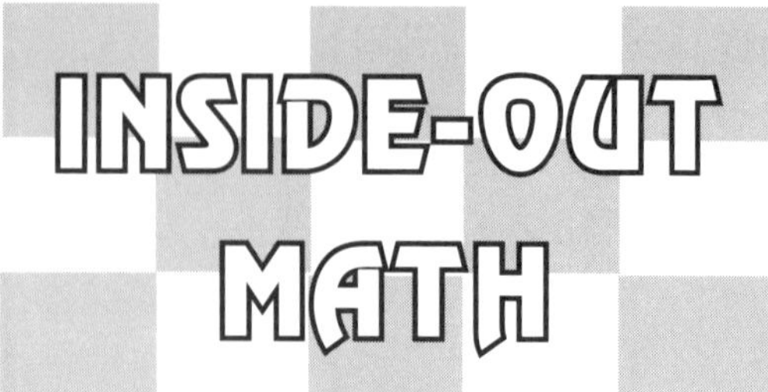

Use the clues to find the missing values.

Problem 1

a: $5\frac{1}{2}$	a+c:	a+d: 12
b:	b-c: $4\frac{1}{2}$	b-d: $2\frac{1}{2}$
	c:	d: ....

Problem 2

a:	a-c: $18\frac{1}{2}$	a-d: $13\frac{1}{2}$
b: $85\frac{1}{2}$	b+c:	b+d: 105
	c:	d: ....

Problem 3

a:	a+c: $1\frac{1}{4}$	a-d: $\frac{1}{4}$
b:	b+c:	b-d: $\frac{1}{2}$
	c: $\frac{3}{4}$	d: ....

Problem 4

a:	a-c: $\frac{2}{3}$	a+d: ....
b:	b-c: $\frac{1}{6}$	b+d: $\frac{3}{4}$
	c:	d: $\frac{1}{4}$

Use the balanced scales to find the missing numbers.

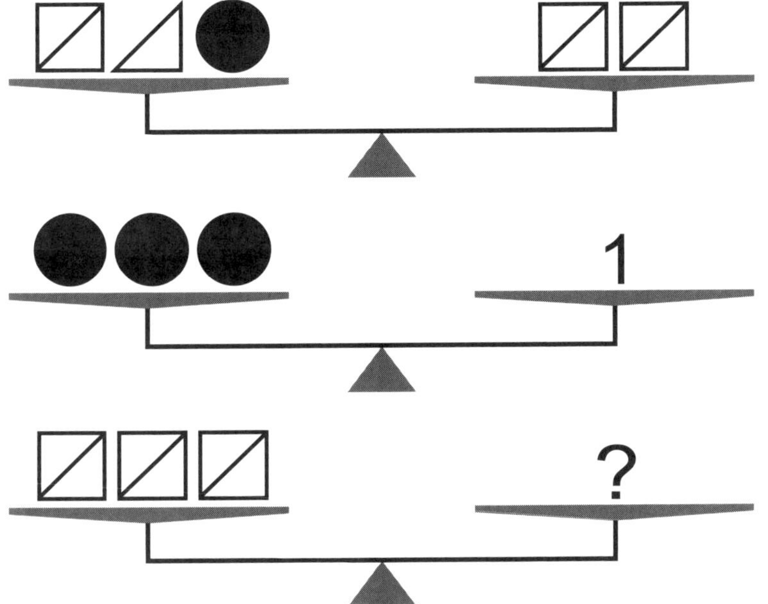

Problem 1

? = ...

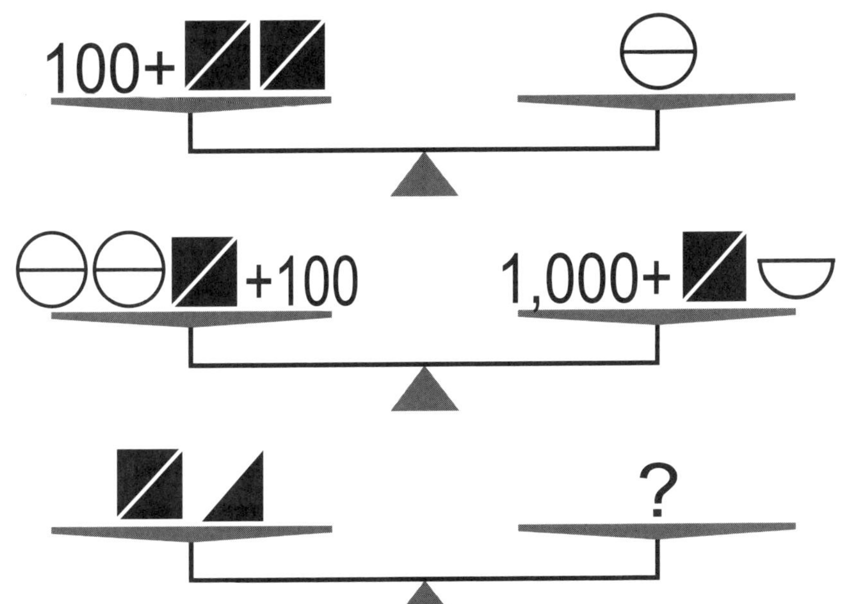

Problem 2

? = ...

All rows, columns, and three numeral diagonals must add up to the same sum. Write the total and then fill in the empty spaces.

Problem 1

		43
	133	
223		169

Total: ....

Problem 2

58		
274		22
112		

Total: ....

Problem 3

		233
	255	343
		189

Total: ....

Problem 4

		279
9	333	657

Total: ....

Use the balanced scales to find the missing numbers.

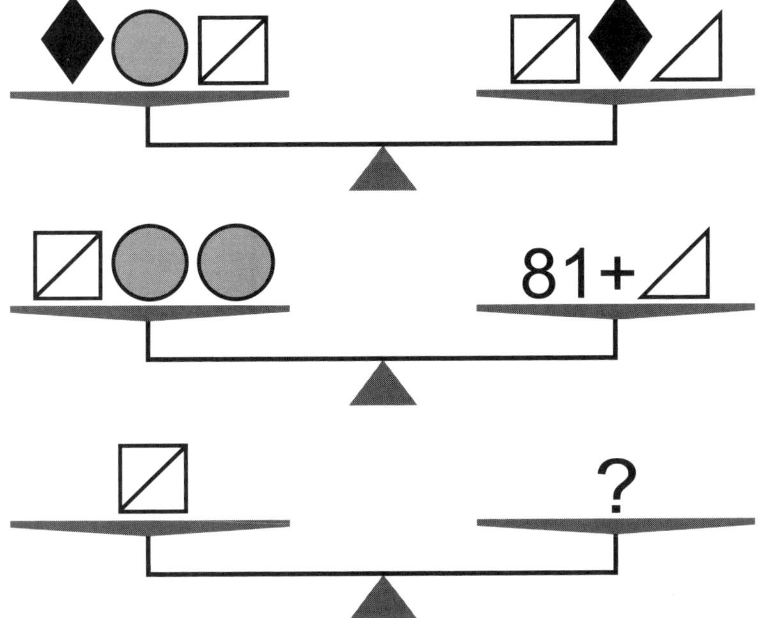

Problem 1

? = ...

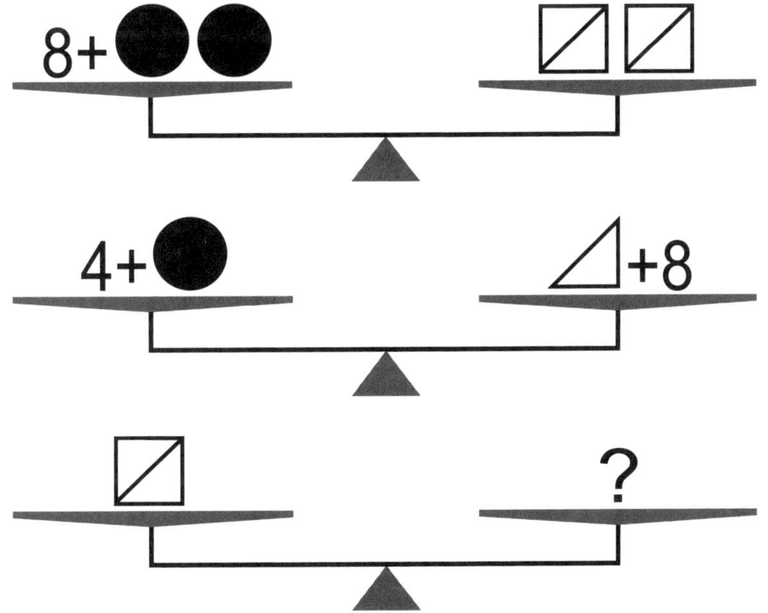

Problem 2

? = ...

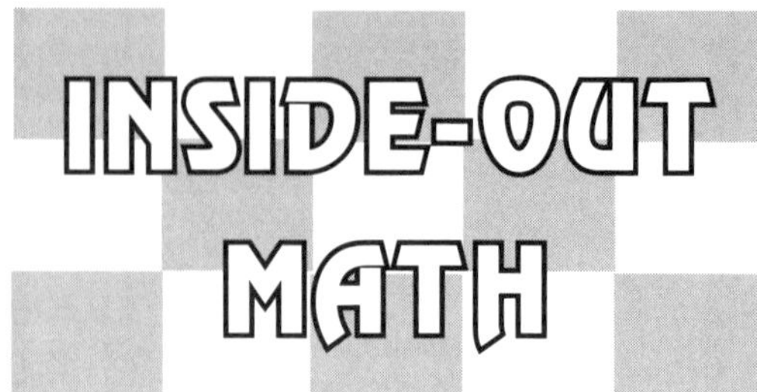

Use the clues to find the missing values.

Problem 1

a: $1\frac{1}{3}$	a+c:	a+d: $6\frac{2}{3}$
b:	b-c: $3\frac{1}{3}$	b-d: $1\frac{2}{3}$
	c:	d: ....

Problem 2

a:	a-c: $\frac{5}{6}$	a-d: $\frac{1}{3}$
b: $1\frac{1}{3}$	b+c: $1\frac{1}{2}$	b+d: ....
	c:	d: ....

Problem 3

a:	a+c: $\frac{7}{8}$	a-d: 0
b:	b+c:	b-d: $\frac{1}{8}$
	c: $\frac{3}{4}$	d: ....

Problem 4

a:	a-c: $\frac{1}{4}$	a+d: ....
b:	b-c: $\frac{2}{3}$	b+d: $1\frac{1}{12}$
	c:	d: $\frac{1}{3}$

Use the balanced scales to find the missing numbers.

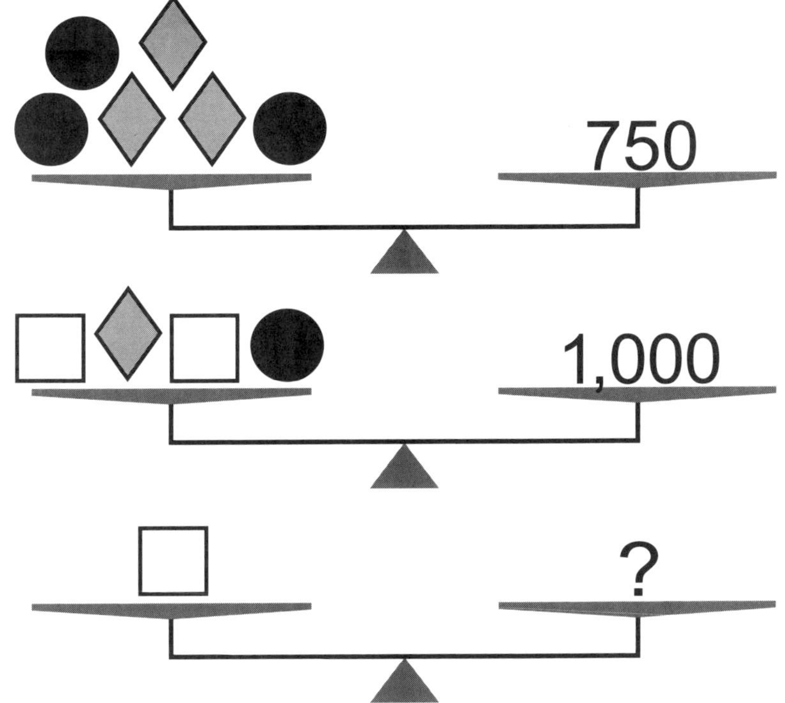

Problem 1

? = ...

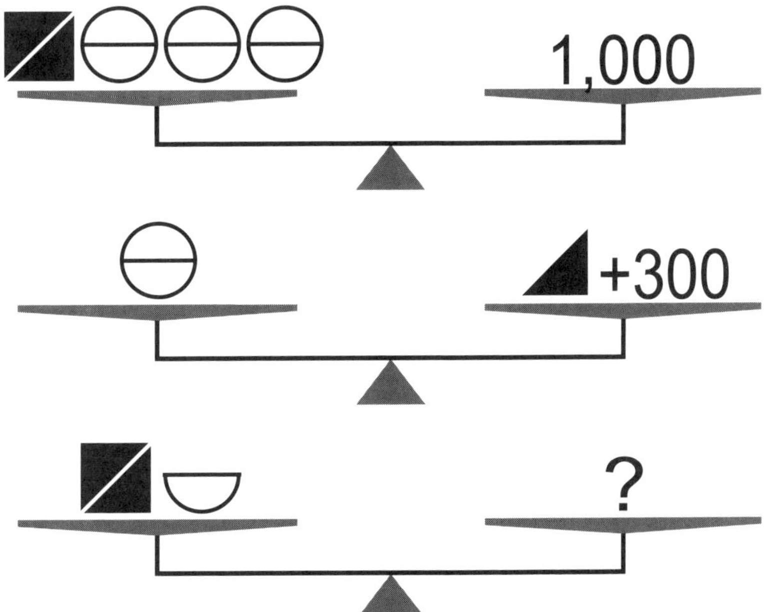

Problem 2

? = ...

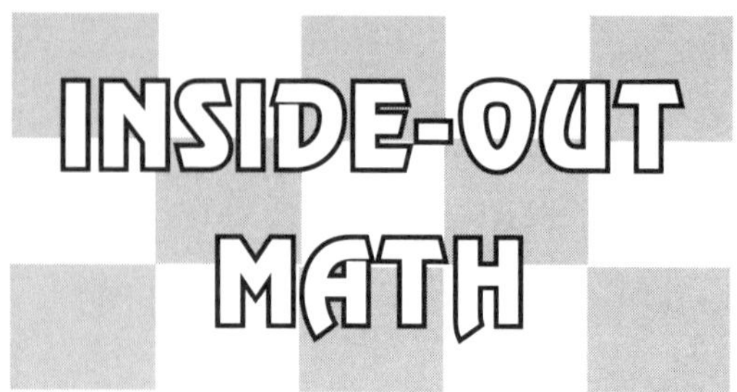

Use the clues to find the missing values.

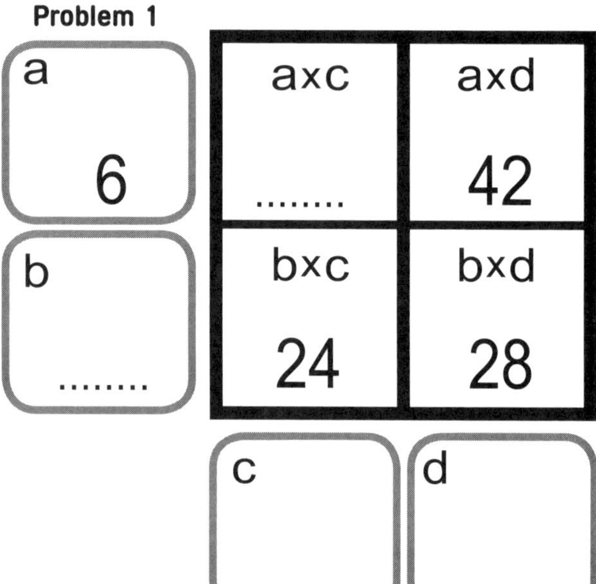

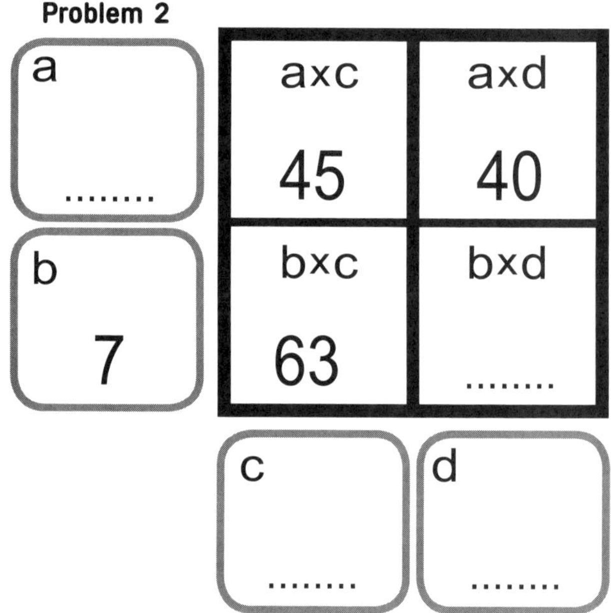

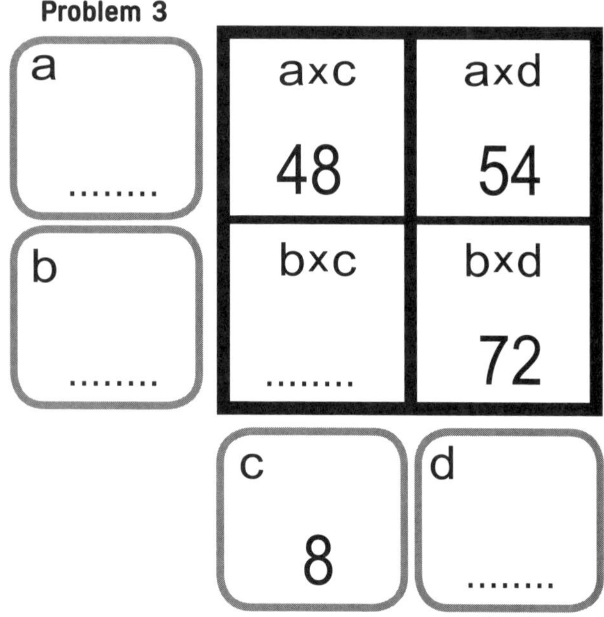

Problem 4

a: ....

b: ....

axc	axd
100	110
bxc	**bxd**
70	....

c: ....

d: 11

All rows, columns, and three numeral diagonals must add up to the same sum. Write the total and then fill in the empty spaces.

Problem 1

4	$1\frac{1}{2}$	2
3		

Total: ....

Problem 2

		3
$1\frac{1}{2}$		$13\frac{1}{2}$
		6

Total: ....

Problem 3

$1\frac{1}{3}$	3	
	$1\frac{2}{3}$	
		2

Total: ....

Problem 4

		$\frac{1}{4}$
$\frac{1}{2}$	1	
$1\frac{3}{4}$		

Total: ....

Use the balanced scales to find the missing numbers.

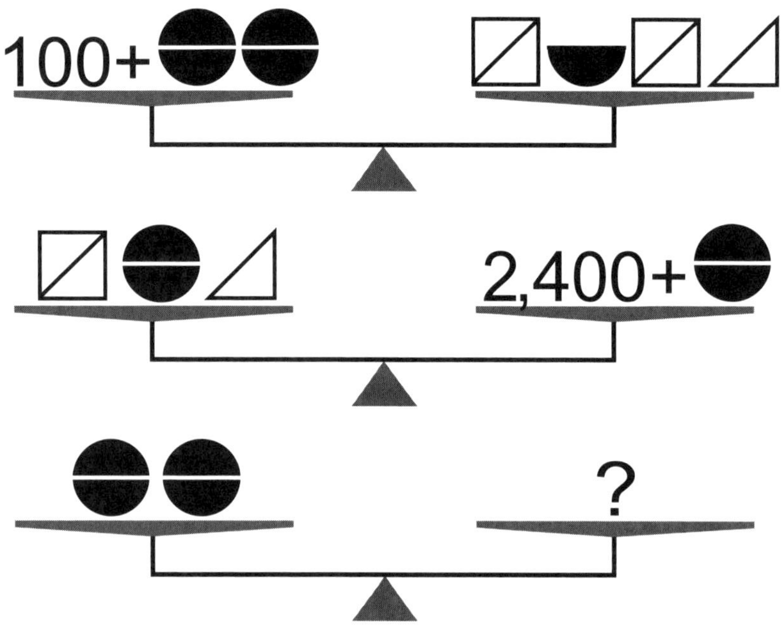

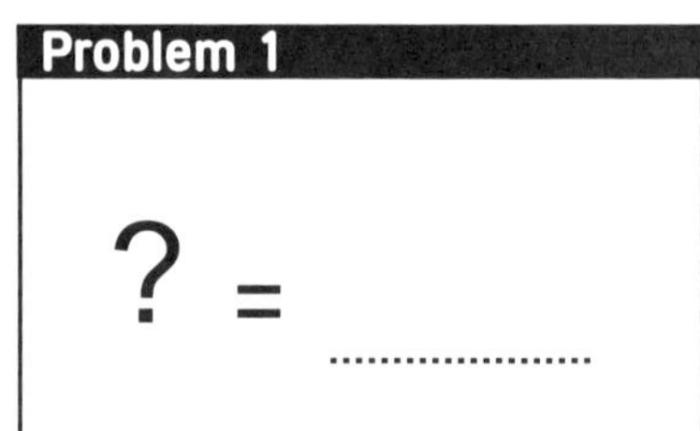

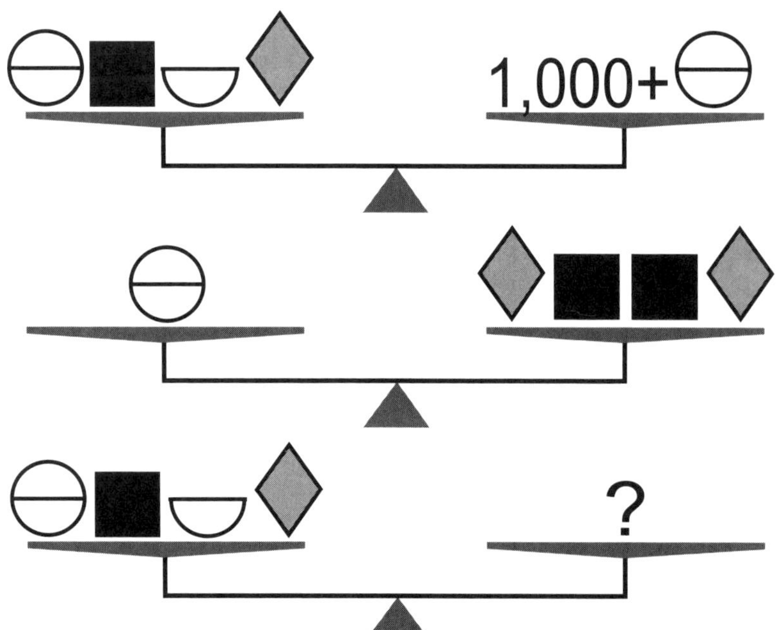

Problem 2

? = ...

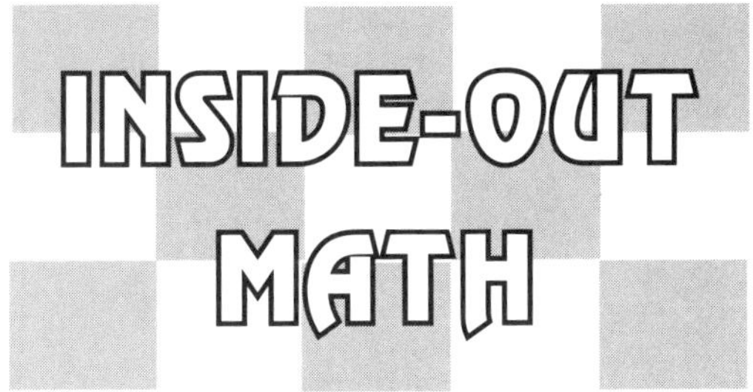

Use the clues to find the missing values.

Problem 1

a: 6
b: ....

	axc	axd
a = 6	....	540
	bxc	bxd
b = ...	560	720

c: ....
d: ....

Problem 2

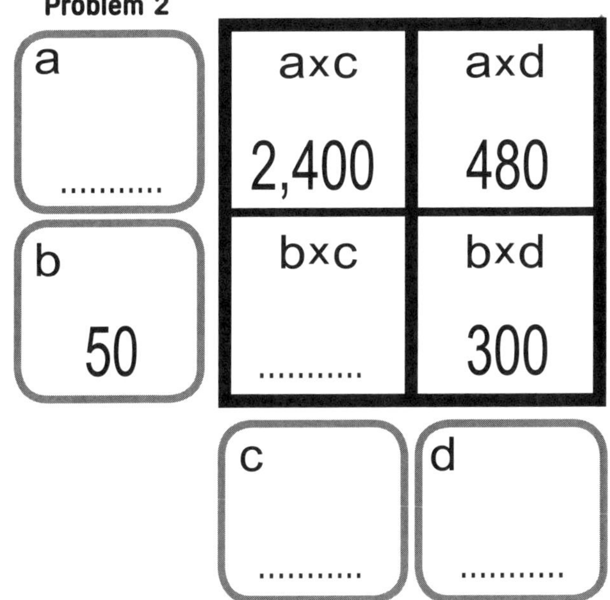

Problem 3

	axc	axd
a = ...	36,000	....
	bxc	bxd
b = ...	20,000	45,000

c: 40
d: ....

Problem 4

	axc	axd
a = ...	1,000	10,000
	bxc	bxd
b = ...	100,000	....

c: ....
d: 1,000

Use the balanced scales to find the missing numbers.

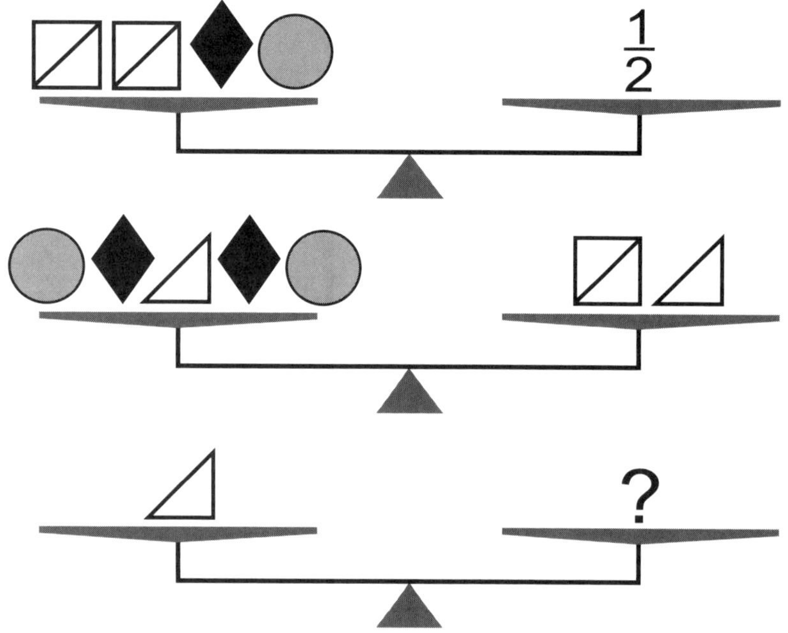

Problem 1

? = ...

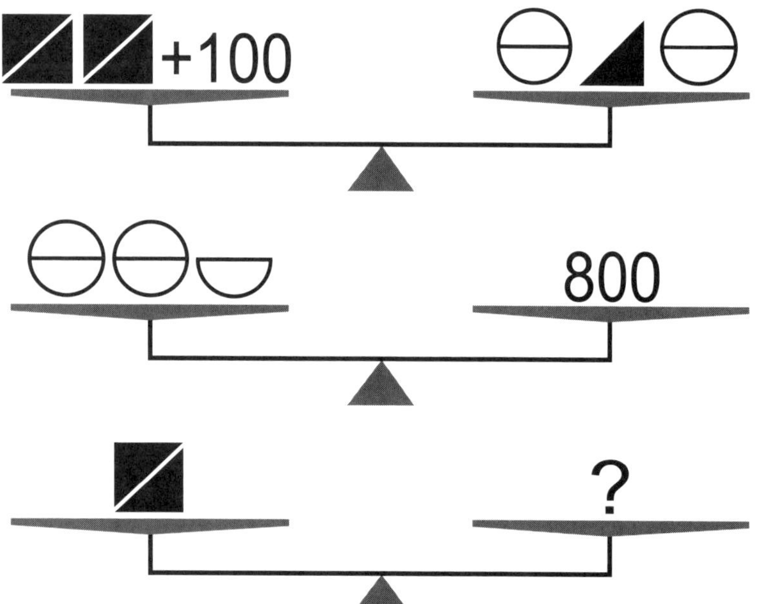

Problem 2

? = ...

All rows, columns, and three numeral diagonals must add up to the same sum. Write the total and then fill in the empty spaces.

Problem 1

	$\frac{1}{5}$	
	1	
	$1\frac{4}{5}$	$\frac{2}{5}$

Total: ....

Problem 2

$\frac{1}{3}$	$1\frac{1}{2}$	$\frac{2}{3}$
		$1\frac{1}{3}$

Total: ....

Problem 3

$\frac{5}{9}$		
$\frac{4}{9}$		
1	$\frac{2}{9}$	

Total: ....

Problem 4

$\frac{1}{12}$	$\frac{1}{2}$	
	$\frac{1}{3}$	
		$\frac{7}{12}$

Total: ....

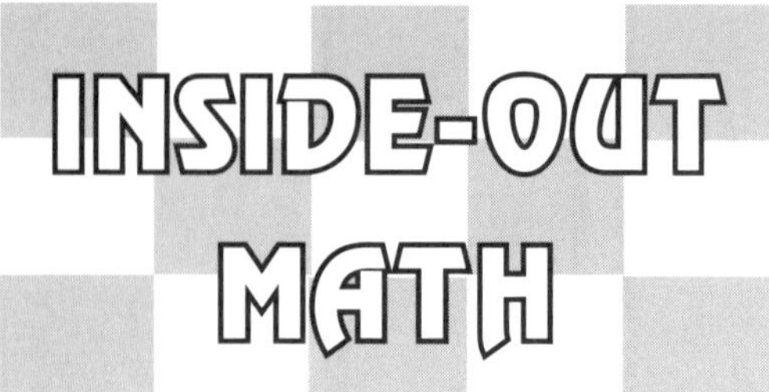

Use the clues to find the missing values.

Problem 1

a	a÷c 6	a÷d 12
b 64	b÷c 8	b÷d ....
	c	d ....

Problem 2

a 240	a÷c	a÷d 40
b	b÷c 120	b÷d 60
	c	d ....

Problem 3

a	a÷c 20	a÷d 10
b	b÷c	b÷d $\frac{1}{2}$
	c 5	d ....

Problem 4

a	a÷c $\frac{1}{2}$	a÷d ....
b	b÷c 1	b÷d 4
	c	d $\frac{1}{2}$

Use the balanced scales to find the missing numbers.

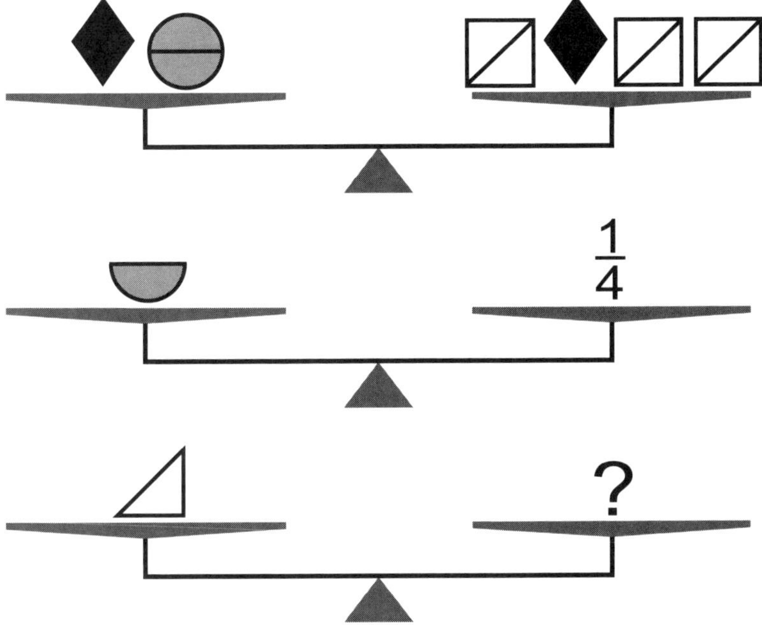

Problem 1

? = ...

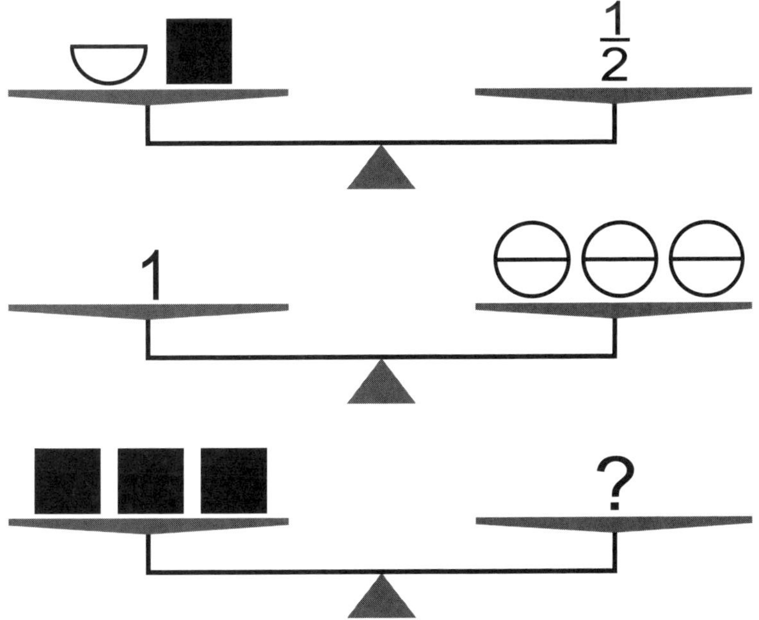

Problem 2

? = ...

Use the balanced scales to find the missing numbers.

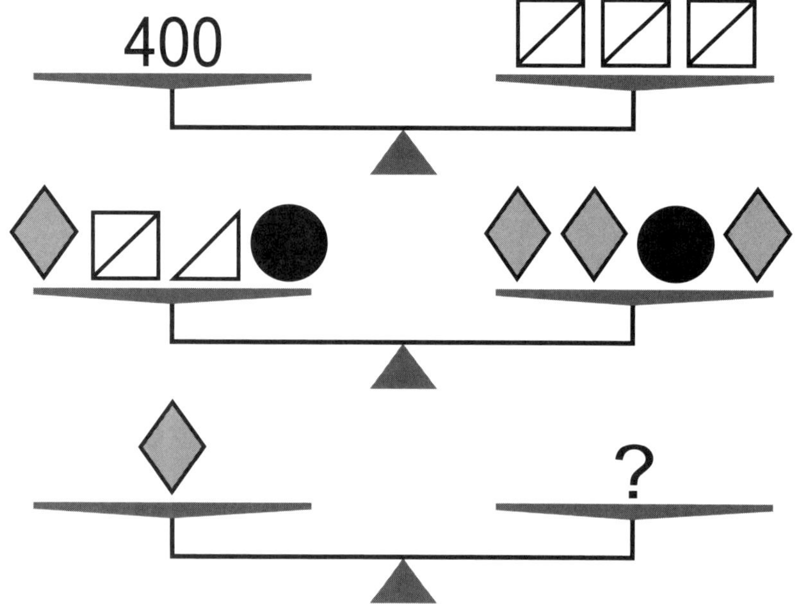

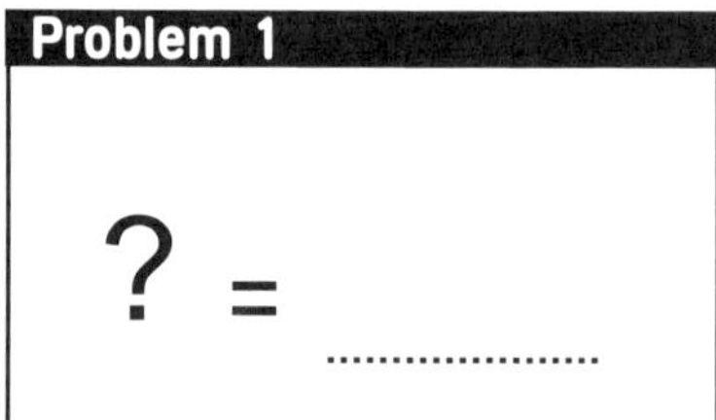

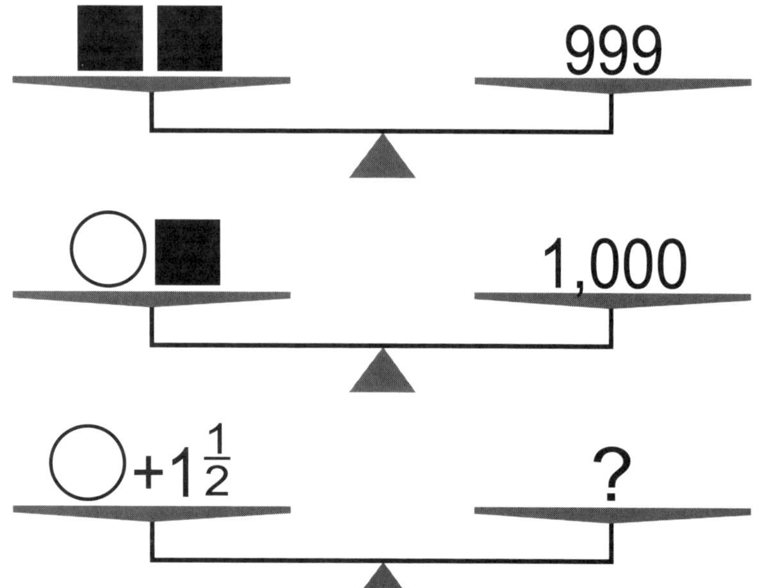

Problem 2

? = ...

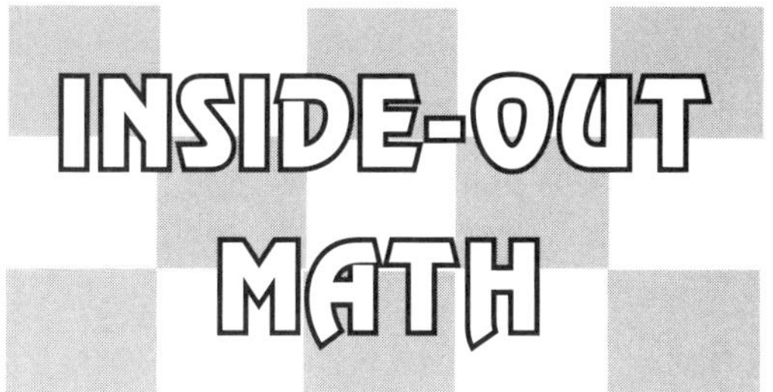

Use the clues to find the missing values.

Problem 1

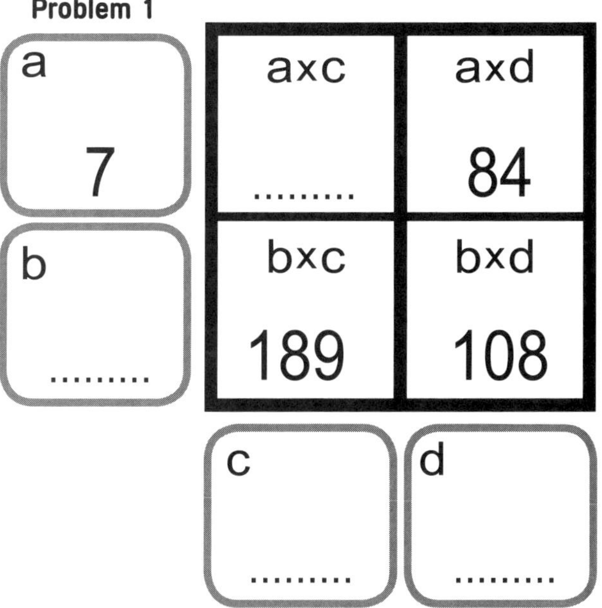

Problem 2

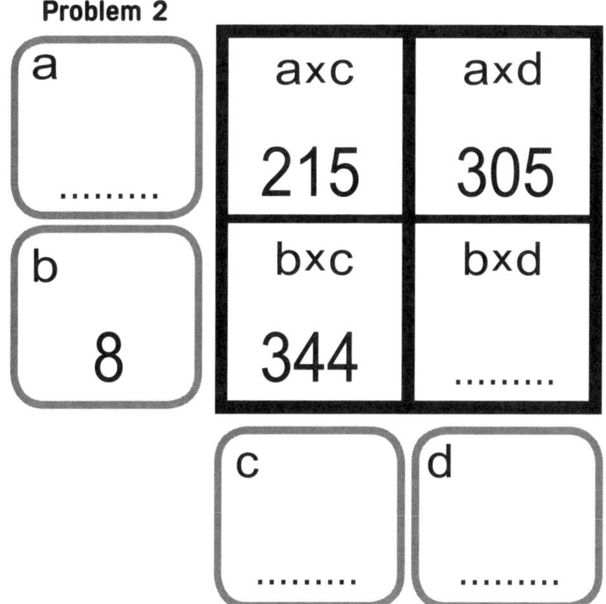

Problem 3

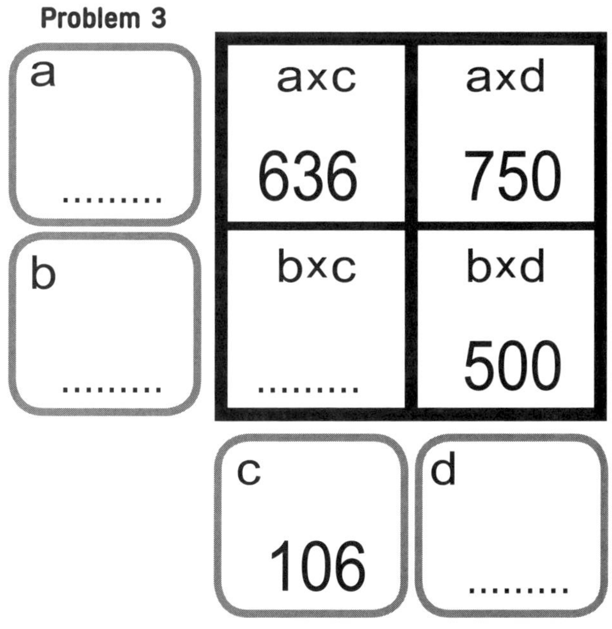

Problem 4

a	axc 3,033	axd ....
b	bxc 8,088	bxd 4,040
	c	d 505

All rows, columns, and three numeral diagonals must add up to the same sum. Write the total and then fill in the empty spaces.

Problem 1

	210	
	1,050	
	1,890	420

Total: ....

Problem 2

8,650		
	6,850	
	13,150	5,050

Total: ....

Problem 3

409		829
	1,039	
1,249		

Total: ....

Problem 4

1		3
	0	
		- 1

Total: ....

Use the balanced scales to find the missing numbers.

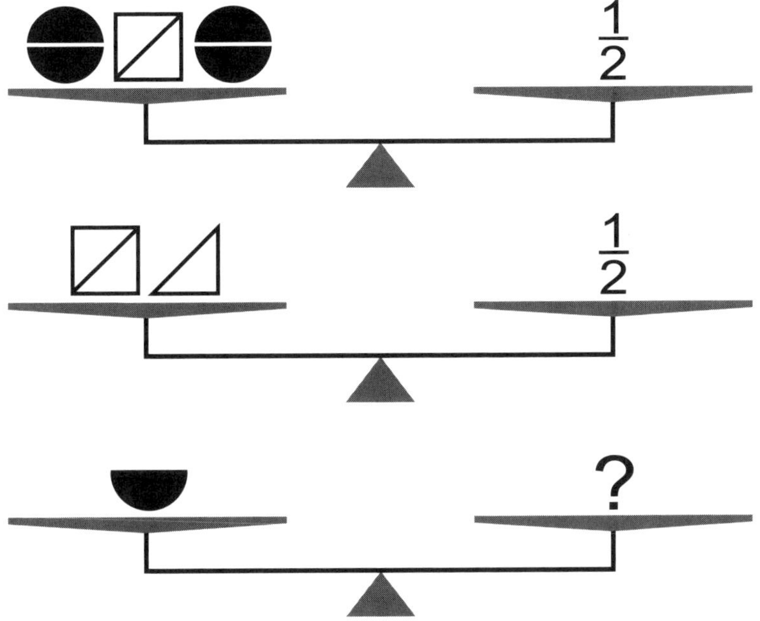

Problem 1

? = ...

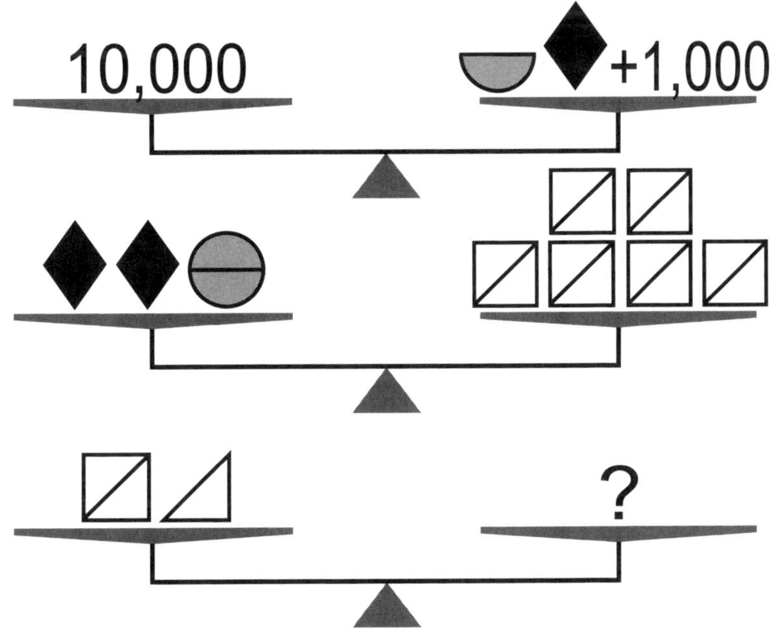

Problem 2

? = ...

BALANCE MATH™ HINTS

Page 1
Problem 1: Divide both sides on 1st balance in half.
Problem 2: Divide both sides on 1st balance in thirds.

Page 2
Problem 1: Divide both sides on 1st balance in half.
Problem 2: Divide both sides on 2nd balance in fourths.

Page 4
Problem 1: Remove ◆ from both sides on 1st balance.
Problem 2: Divide both sides on 1st balance in half.

Page 6
Problem 1: Remove ◇ from both sides on 2nd balance.
Problem 2: Divide both sides on 1st balance in half.

Page 7
Problem 1: Divide both sides on 1st balance in thirds.
Problem 2: Remove ■ from both sides on 2nd balance.

Page 10
Problem 1: Remove ◆ from both sides on 1st balance.
Problem 2: Divide both sides on 1st balance in half.

Page 12
Problem 1: Divide both sides on 1st balance in half.
Problem 2: Divide both sides on 1st balance in thirds.

Page 13
Problem 1: Divide both sides on 1st balance in fourths.
Problem 2: Divide both sides on 2nd balance in thirds.

Page 15
Problem 1: Remove 100 from both sides on 1st balance.
Problem 2: Divide both sides on 1st balance in fifths.

Page 17
Problem 1: Remove ● from both sides on 2nd balance.
Problem 2: Divide both sides on 2nd balance in half.

Page 18
Problem 1: Remove ■ ⊖ from both sides on 2nd balance.
Problem 2: Remove ◆◆ from both sides on 2nd balance.

Page 21
Problem 1: Remove ■ from both sides on 1st balance.
Problem 2: Divide both sides on 1st balance in half.

Page 23
Problem 1: Remove ⧄ ◺ from both side on 1st balance.
Problem 2: Remove ◩ ◡ + 100 from both sides on 2nd balance.

Page 25
Problem 1: Remove ◆ ⧄ from both sides on 1st balance.
Problem 2: Divide both sides on 1st balance in half.

Page 27
Problem 1: Divide both sides on 1st balance in thirds.
Problem 2: Substitute ◢ + 300 from 2nd balance for ⊖ on 1st balance.

Page 30
Problem 1: Remove ⊖ from both sides on 2nd balance.
Problem 2: Divide both sides on 2nd balance in half.

Page 32
Problem 1: Remove ◺ from both sides on 2nd balance.
Problem 2: Divide both sides on 2nd balance in fifths.

Page 35
Problem 1: Double both sides on 2nd balance.
Problem 2: Divide both sides on 2nd balance in sixths.

Page 36
Problem 1: Divide both sides on 1st balance in half.
Problem 2: Divide both sides on 1st balance in half.

Page 39
Problem 1: Divide both sides on 2nd balance in thirds.
Problem 2: Double both sides on 1st balance.

ANSWERS

Page 1

Problem 1: ? = 80

Explanation: Divide both sides on 1st balance in half so ○ = 15. Substitute 15 for ○ on 2nd balance so 15 + ■ = 55. Remove 15 from both sides so ■ = 40. ■■ = 40 + 40 = 80.

Problem 2: ? = 15

Explanation: Divide both sides on 1st balance in thirds so ★ = 9. Substitute 9 for ★ on 2nd balance so 9 + 9 = 18 = ◇◇◇. Divide both sides in thirds so ◇ = 6. ◇★ = 6 + 9 = 15.

Page 2

Problem 1: ? = 75

Explanation: Divide both sides on 1st balance in half, so ○ = 50. Substitute 50 for ○ on 2nd balance so ★★ + 50 = 100. Remove 50 from both sides so ★★ = 50. Divide both sides in half so ★ = 25. ★★★ = 25 + 25 + 25 = 75

Problem 2: ? = 9

Explanation: Divide both sides on 2nd balance in fourths so ◆ = 8. Substitute 8 for each ◆ on 1st balance so ⧄⧄⧄⧄ = 8 + 8 + 8 + 8 = 32. Divide both sides in fourths so ⧄ = 6. Divide in half so ◿ = 3. ⧄◿ = 6 + 3 = 9.

Page 3

Problem 1: b = 60
c = 40
d = 20
a + d = 30

Problem 2: a = 90
c = 60
d = 30
b + d = 80

Problem 3: a = 15
b = 35
d = 95
a + c = 80

Problem 4: a = 50
b = 200
c = 75
b + d = 225

Page 4

Problem 1: ? = 90

Explanation: Remove ◆ from both sides on 1st balance so ▩▩ = ⊖. Divide both sides on 2nd balance in thirds so ▩ = 30. Substitute 30 for each ▩ on 1st balance so 30 + 30 = 60 = ⊖. Divide in half so ◡ = 30. ⊖◡ = 60 + 30 = 90.

Problem 2: ? = 125

Explanation: Divide both sides on 1st balance in half so ☆■ = 15. Substitute 15 for ☆■ on 2nd balance so 15 + ◍ = 40. Remove 15 from both sides so ◍ = 25. ◍◍◍◍◍ = 25 + 25 + 25 + 25 + 25 = 125.

Page 5

Problem 1:

16	6	8
2	10	18
12	14	4

Total: 30

Problem 2:

10	15	14
17	13	9
12	11	16

Total: 39

Problem 3:

10	9	11
11	10	9
9	11	10

Total: 30

Problem 4:

20	90	40
70	50	30
60	10	80

Total: 150

Page 6

Problem 1: ? = 135

Explanation: Remove ◇ from both sides on 2nd balance so ●● = 70. Divide both sides in half so ● = 35. Substitute 35 for ● on 1st balance so ◇ + 35 = 80. Remove 35 from both sides so ◇ = 45. ◇◇◇ = 45 + 45 + 45 = 135.

Problem 2: ? = 15

Explanation: Divide both sides on 1st balance in half so ⊖⊖ = ⧄. Substitute ⊖⊖ for ⧄ on 2nd balance so 5 + ⊖⊖⊖⊖ = 45. Remove 5 from both sides so ⊖⊖⊖⊖ = 40. Divide both sides in eighths so ◡ = 5. Substitute 40 for ⊖⊖⊖⊖ on 1st balance so 40 = ⧄⧄. Divide in fourths so ◿ = 10. ◡◿ = 5 + 10 = 15.

Page 7

Problem 1: ? = 45

Explanation: Divide both sides on 1st balance in thirds so ◿ = 8. Substitute 8 for each ◿ on 2nd balance so 8 + 8 + 8 + 8 = 32 = ◆◆ + 2. Remove 2 from both sides so 30 = ◆◆. Divide both sides in half so 15 = ◆. ◆◆◆ = 15 + 15 + 15 = 45.

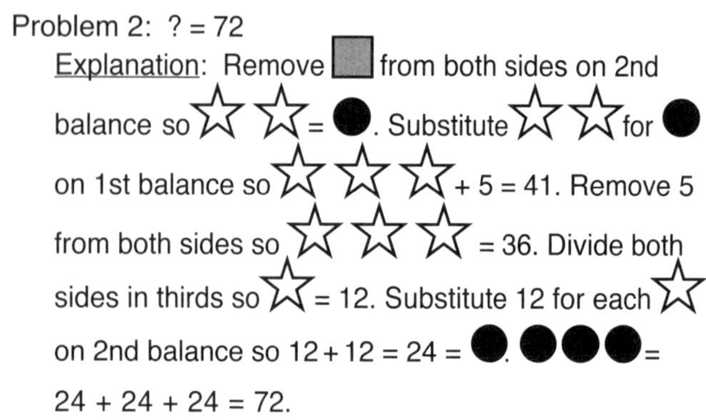
Problem 2: ? = 72
Explanation: Remove ■ from both sides on 2nd balance so ☆☆ = ●. Substitute ☆☆ for ● on 1st balance so ☆☆☆ + 5 = 41. Remove 5 from both sides so ☆☆☆ = 36. Divide both sides in thirds so ☆ = 12. Substitute 12 for each ☆ on 2nd balance so 12 + 12 = 24 = ●. ●●● = 24 + 24 + 24 = 72.

Page 8

Problem 1: b = 64, c = 29, d = 37, a + d = 74

Problem 2: a = 86, c = 59, d = 98, b + d = 175

Problem 3: a = 219, b = 137, d = 184, a + c = 475

Problem 4: a = 130, b = 370, c = 880, b + c = 1,250

Page 9

Problem 1:

45	35	85
95	55	15
25	75	65

Total: 165

Problem 2:

111	134	124
136	123	110
122	112	135

Total: 369

Problem 3:

60	80	160
200	100	0
40	120	140

Total: 300

Problem 4:

51	9	39
21	33	45
27	57	15

Total: 99

Page 10

Problem 1: ? = 100
Explanation: Remove ◆ from both sides on 1st balance so ⊖◪ = 120. Divide both sides on 2nd balance in thirds so ⊖ = ◺. Substitute ⊖ for each ◺ above so ⊖⊖⊖ = 120. Divide in sixths so ◡ = 20. Substitute 20 for each ◡ so 20 + 20 = 40 = ◺ and ◪ = 80. ◡◪ = 20 + 80 = 100.

Problem 2: ? = 5
Explanation: Divide both sides on 1st balance in half so ◼◇ = 75. Substitute 75 for ◼◇ on 2nd balance so ◢ + 75 = 110. Remove 75 from both sides so ◢ = 35. Double both sides so ◼ = 70. Substitute 70 for ◼ above so 70 + ◇ = 75. Remove 70 from both sides so ◇ = 5.

Page 11

Problem 1: b = 80, c = 30, d = 50, a - d = 60

Problem 2: a = 750, c = 160, d = 380, b - d = 430

Problem 3: a = 93, b = 81, d = 36, a - c = 66

Problem 4: a = 167, b = 214, c = 81, b - d = 113

Page 12

Problem 1: ? = 11
Explanation: Divide both sides on 1st balance in half so ◇ = $1\frac{1}{2}$. Substitute $1\frac{1}{2}$ for ◇ on 2nd balance so $1\frac{1}{2}$ + ● = 7. Remove $1\frac{1}{2}$ from both sides so ● = $5\frac{1}{2}$. ●● = $5\frac{1}{2} + 5\frac{1}{2}$ = 11.

Problem 2: ? = 1
Explanation: Divide both sides on 1st balance in thirds so ★ = $\frac{1}{3}$. Substitute $\frac{1}{3}$ for ★ on 2nd balance so 1 = ◪ + $\frac{1}{3}$. Remove $\frac{1}{3}$ from both sides so $\frac{2}{3}$ = ◪. Divide both sides in half so ◺ = $\frac{1}{3}$. So ◪◺ = $\frac{1}{3} + \frac{1}{3} + \frac{1}{3}$ = 1.

Page 13

Problem 1: ? = $\frac{1}{2}$
Explanation: Divide both sides on 1st balance in fourth so ◇ = 13. Substitute 13 for ◇ on 2nd balance so 13 + 13 + 13 + ■■ = 40. Remove 39 from both sides so ■■ = 1. Divide both sides in half so ■ = $\frac{1}{2}$.

Problem 2: ? = $1\frac{1}{4}$
Explanation: Divide both sides on 2nd balance in thirds so ◺ = ⊖. Divide both sides on 1st balance in fourths so ◺ = $2\frac{1}{2}$. Substitute $2\frac{1}{2}$ for ◺ above so $2\frac{1}{2}$ = ⊖. Divide both sides in half so ◡ = $1\frac{1}{4}$.

Page 14

Problem 1: b = 84, c = 37, d = 55, a - d = 37

Problem 2: a = 125, c = 86, d = 78, b - d = 54

Problem 3: a = 403, b = 307, d = 189, a - c = 255

Problem 4: a = 8,700, b = 9,320, c = 1,350, b - d = 4,550

Page 15

Problem 1: ? = 700

Explanation: Remove 100 from both sides on 1st balance so ○ = 125. Substitute 125 for each ○ on 2nd balance so 125 + 125 + ■ = 600. Remove 250 from both sides so ■ = 350. ■ ■ = 350 + 350 = 700.

Problem 2: ? = $\frac{3}{4}$

Explanation: Divide both sides on 1st balance in fifths so ◺ = 6. Substitute 6 for ◺ on 2nd balance so 6 = ⊖⊖⊖⊖. Divide both sides in fourths so $1\frac{1}{2}$ = ⊖. ◡ = $\frac{3}{4}$.

Page 16

Problem 1:

480	60	360
180	300	420
240	540	120

Total: 900

Problem 2:

65	215	185
275	155	35
125	95	245

Total: 465

Problem 3:

60	100	44
52	68	84
92	36	76

Total: 204

Problem 4:

109	7	103
67	73	79
43	139	37

Total: 219

Page 17

Problem 1: ? = 200

Explanation: Remove ● from both sides on 2nd balance so ⧄ ◺ = 450. Divide both sides in thirds so ◺ = 150. Double both side so ⧄ = 300. Substitute 300 for ⧄ on 1st balance so 500 = 300 + ◇. Remove 300 from both sides so ◇ = 200.

Problem 2: ? = 250

Explanation: Divide both sides on 2nd balance in half so ◆ = ⊖ ◡. Substitute ⊖ ◡ for ◆ on 1st balance so ⊖⊖⊖◡ = 350. Divide both sides in sevenths so ◡ = 50. Double both sides so ⊖ = 100. Substitute 50 for each ◡ above so ◆ = 150. ◆⊖ = 150 + 100 = 250.

Page 18

Problem 1: ? = 111

Explanation: Remove ■⊖ from both sides on 2nd balance so ⊖ ◡ = ◆ ◆. Divide both sides on 1st balance in thirds so ◆ = 333. Substitute 333 for each ◆ so ⊖ ◡ = 333 + 333 = 666. Divide both sides in thirds so ◡ = 222. Double both sides so ⊖ = 444.

Problem 2: ? = 270

Explanation: Remove ◇◇ from both sides on 2nd balance so ⧄● = ◇ + 10. Substitute ◇ + 10 for ⧄● on 1st balance so ◇ + 10 = 100. Remove 10 from both sides so ◇ = 90. ◇◇◇ = 90 + 90 + 90 = 270.

Page 19

Problem 1: b = 11,900
c = 14,800
d = 10,900
a + c = 25,000

Problem 2: a = 1,222
c = 9,889
d = 9,879
b + d = 10,990

Problem 3: a = 3,751
b = 5,063
d = 3,978
b + c = 9,922

Problem 4: a = 8,365
b = 7,946
c = 2,737
a + d = 14,260

Page 20

Problem 1:

129	3	201
183	111	39
21	219	93

Total: 333

Problem 2:

163	118	127
100	136	172
145	154	109

Total: 408

Problem 3:

160	105	116
83	127	171
138	149	94

Total: 381

Problem 4:

124	292	28
52	148	244
268	4	172

Total: 444

Page 21

Problem 1: ? = 100

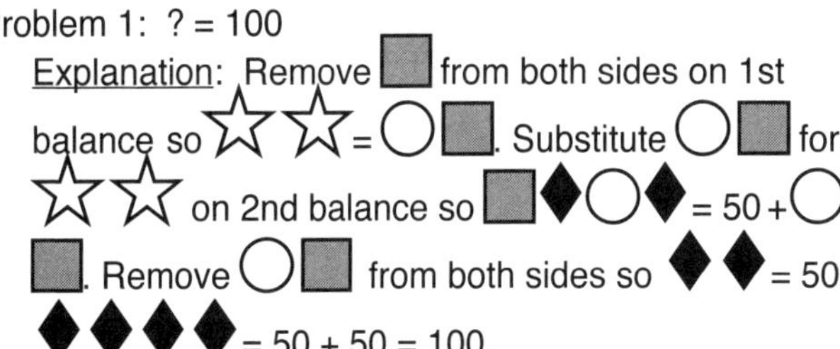

Explanation: Remove ■ from both sides on 1st balance so ☆☆ = ○■. Substitute ○■ for ☆☆ on 2nd balance so ■◆○◆ = 50 + ○■. Remove ○■ from both sides so ◆◆ = 50. ◆◆◆◆ = 50 + 50 = 100.

Problem 2: ? = 2,000

<u>Explanation</u>: Divide both sides on 1st balance in half so ■◢ = ○★. Substitute ■◢ for ★○ on 2nd balance so 1,000 = ■◢ + 250. Remove 250 from both sides so 750 = ■◢. Divide both sides into thirds so 250 = ◢. Double both sides so 500 = ■. ■■■■ = 500 + 500 + 500 + 500 = 2,000.

Page 22

Problem 1: b = 9, c = $4\frac{1}{2}$, d = $6\frac{1}{2}$, a + c = 10

Problem 2: a = 33, c = $14\frac{1}{2}$, d = $19\frac{1}{2}$, b + c = 100

Problem 3: a = $\frac{1}{2}$, b = $\frac{3}{4}$, d = $\frac{1}{4}$, b + c = $1\frac{1}{2}$

Problem 4: a = 1, b = $\frac{1}{2}$, c = $\frac{1}{3}$, a + d = $1\frac{1}{4}$

Page 23

Problem 1: ? = 2

<u>Explanation</u>: Remove ⧄◿ from both sides on 1st balance so ● = ◿. Substitute ◿ for each ● on 2nd balance so ◿◿◿ = 1. Double both sides so ⧄⧄⧄ = 1 x 2 = 2.

Problem 2: ? = 375

<u>Explanation</u>: Remove ◪◡ + 100 from both sides on 2nd balance so ⊖◡ = 900. Divide both sides in thirds so ◡ = 300. Double both sides so ⊖ = 600. Substitute 600 for ⊖ on 1st balance so 100 + ◪◪ = 600. Remove 100 from both sides so ◪◪ = 500. Divide both sides in fourths so ◢ = 125. ◪◢ = 125 x 3 = 375.

Page 24

Problem 1:

97	259	43
79	133	187
223	7	169

Total: 399

Problem 2:

58	202	184
274	148	22
112	94	238

Total: 444

Problem 3:

321	211	233
167	255	343
277	299	189

Total: 765

Problem 4:

603	117	279
9	333	657
387	549	63

Total: 999

Page 25

Problem 1: ? = 54

<u>Explanation</u>: Remove ◆⧄ from both sides on 1st balance so ◍ = ◿. Substitute ◿ for ◍ on 2nd balance so ⧄◿◿ = 81 + ◿. Remove ◿ from both sides so ⧄◿ = 81. Divide both sides in thirds so ◿ = 27. ⧄ = 27 x 2 = 54.

Problem 2: ? = 16

<u>Explanation</u>: Divide both sides on 1st balance in half so 4 + ● = ⧄. Substitute ⧄ for 4 + ● on 2nd balance so ⧄ = ◿ + 8. Remove ◿ from both sides so ◿ = 8. ⧄ = 8 x 2 = 16.

Page 26

Problem 1: b = 7, c = $3\frac{2}{3}$, d = $5\frac{1}{3}$, a + c = 5

Problem 2: a = 1, c = $\frac{1}{6}$, d = $\frac{2}{3}$, b + d = 2

Problem 3: a = $\frac{1}{8}$, b = $\frac{1}{4}$, d = $\frac{1}{8}$, b + c = 1

Problem 4: a = $\frac{1}{3}$, b = $\frac{3}{4}$, c = $\frac{1}{12}$, a + d = $\frac{2}{3}$

Page 27

Problem 1: ? = 375

<u>Explanation</u>: Divide both sides on 1st balance in thirds so ◈● = 250. Substitute 250 for ◈● on 2nd balance so □□ + 250 = 1,000. Remove 250 from both sides so □□ = 750. Divide both sides in half so □ = 375.

Problem 2: ? = 200

<u>Explanation</u>: Substitute ◢ + 300 from 2nd balance for each ⊖ on 1st balance so ◪◪◢ + 900 = 1,000. Remove 900 from both sides so ◪◪◢ = 100. Divide both sides in fifths so ◢ = 20. Substitute 20 for ◢ on 2nd balance so ⊖ = 20 + 300. Divide both sides in half so ◡ = 160. ◪◡ = 40 + 160 = 200.

Page 28

Problem 1: b = 4, c = 6, d = 7, a x c = 36

Problem 2: a = 5, c = 9, d = 8, b x d = 56

Problem 3: a = 6, b = 8, d = 9, b x c = 64

Problem 4: a = 10, b = 7, c = 10, b x d = 77

Page 29

Problem 1:

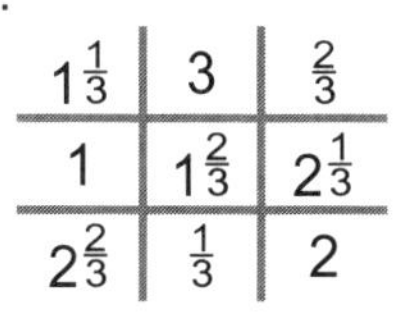

4	$1\frac{1}{2}$	2
$\frac{1}{2}$	$2\frac{1}{2}$	$4\frac{1}{2}$
3	$3\frac{1}{2}$	1

Total: $7\frac{1}{2}$

Problem 2:

9	$10\frac{1}{2}$	3
$1\frac{1}{2}$	$7\frac{1}{2}$	$13\frac{1}{2}$
12	$4\frac{1}{2}$	6

Total: $22\frac{1}{2}$

Problem 3:

$1\frac{1}{3}$	3	$\frac{2}{3}$
1	$1\frac{2}{3}$	$2\frac{1}{3}$
$2\frac{2}{3}$	$\frac{1}{3}$	2

Total: 5

Problem 4:

$\frac{3}{4}$	2	$\frac{1}{4}$
$\frac{1}{2}$	1	$1\frac{1}{2}$
$1\frac{3}{4}$	0	$1\frac{1}{4}$

Total: 3

Page 30

Problem 1: ? = 5,200

Explanation: Remove from both sides on 2nd balance so = 2,400. Divide both sides in thirds so = 800. Substitute 800 for each on 1st balance so 100 + = + 800 + 800 + 800 + 800 + 800. Remove 100 + from both sides so = 3,900. Divide in thirds so = 1,300. = 1,300 x 4 = 5,200

Problem 2: ? = 2,000

Explanation: Divide both sides on 2nd balance in half so = . Substitute for on 1st balance so = 1,000 + . Remove from both sides so = 1,000. Divide above in half so = 500. Substitute 1,000 for on 2nd balance so = 1,000. Divide in half so = 500. = 1,000 + 500 + 500 = 2,000.

Page 31

Problem 1: b = 8
c = 70
d = 90
a x c = 420

Problem 2: a = 80
c = 3
d = 60
b x c = 150

Problem 3: a = 900
b = 500
d = 90
a x d = 81,000

Problem 4: a = 10
b = 1,000
c = 100
b x d = 1,000,000

Page 32

Problem 1: ? = $\frac{1}{10}$

Explanation: Remove from both sides on 2nd balance so = . Divide both sides in half so = . Substitute for on 1st balance so = $\frac{1}{2}$. Divide both sides into fifths so = $\frac{1}{10}$.

Problem 2: ? = 360

Explanation: Divide both sides on 2nd balance in fifths so = 160. Double so = 320. Substitute 320 for each on 1st balance so + 100 = + 320 + 320. Remove 100 + from both sides so = 540. Divide both sides in thirds so = 180. = 180 x 2 = 360.

Page 33

Problem 1:

$1\frac{3}{5}$	$\frac{1}{5}$	$1\frac{1}{5}$
$\frac{3}{5}$	1	$1\frac{2}{5}$
$\frac{4}{5}$	$1\frac{4}{5}$	$\frac{2}{5}$

Total: 3

Problem 2:

$\frac{1}{3}$	$1\frac{1}{2}$	$\frac{2}{3}$
$1\frac{1}{6}$	$\frac{5}{6}$	$\frac{1}{2}$
1	$\frac{1}{6}$	$1\frac{1}{3}$

Total: $2\frac{1}{2}$

Problem 3:

$\frac{5}{9}$	$1\frac{1}{9}$	$\frac{1}{3}$
$\frac{4}{9}$	$\frac{2}{3}$	$\frac{8}{9}$
1	$\frac{2}{9}$	$\frac{7}{9}$

Total: 2

Problem 4:

$\frac{1}{12}$	$\frac{1}{2}$	$\frac{5}{12}$
$\frac{2}{3}$	$\frac{1}{3}$	0
$\frac{1}{4}$	$\frac{1}{6}$	$\frac{7}{12}$

Total: 1

Page 34

Problem 1: a = 48
c = 8
d = 4
b ÷ d = 16

Problem 2: b = 360
c = 3
d = 6
a ÷ c = 80

Problem 3: a = 100
b = 5
d = 10
b ÷ c = 1

Problem 4: a = 1
b = 2
c = 2
a ÷ d = 2

Page 35

Problem 1: ? = $\frac{1}{12}$

Explanation: Double both sides on 2nd balance so = $\frac{1}{2}$. Substitute $\frac{1}{2}$ for on 1st balance so + $\frac{1}{2}$ = . Remove both sides so $\frac{1}{2}$ = . Divide both sides in thirds so $\frac{1}{6}$ = . Divide both sides in half so = $\frac{1}{12}$.

Problem 2: ? = 1

Explanation: Divide both sides on 2nd balance in sixths so $\frac{1}{6}$ = . Substitute $\frac{1}{6}$ for on 1st balance so $\frac{1}{6}$ + = $\frac{1}{2}$. Remove $\frac{1}{6}$ from both sides so = $\frac{2}{6}$ or $\frac{1}{3}$. = $\frac{1}{3} + \frac{1}{3} + \frac{1}{3} = 1$.

Page 36

Problem 1: ? = 100

Explanation: Divide both sides on 1st balance in half so 200 = . Substitute 200 for on 2nd balance so + 200 + = . Remove from both so 200 = . Divide both sides in half so = 100.

Problem 2: ? = 502

Explanation: Divide both sides on 1st balance in half so = $499\frac{1}{2}$. Substitute $499\frac{1}{2}$ for on 2nd balance so $499\frac{1}{2}$ + = 1,000. Remove $499\frac{1}{2}$ from both sides so = $500\frac{1}{2}$. + $1\frac{1}{2}$ = 502.

Page 37

Problem 1: b = 9
c = 21
d = 12
a x c = 147

Problem 2: a = 5
c = 43
d = 61
b x d = 488

Problem 3: a = 6
b = 4
d = 125
b x c = 424

Problem 4: a = 3
b = 8
c = 1,011
a x d = 1,515

Page 38

Problem 1:

1,680	210	1,260
630	1,050	1,470
840	1,890	420

Total: 3,150

Problem 2:

8,650	550	11,350
9,550	6,850	4,150
2,350	13,150	5,050

Total: 20,550

Problem 3:

409	1,879	829
1,459	1,039	619
1,249	199	1,669

Total: 3,117

Problem 4:

1	-4	3
2	0	-2
-3	4	-1

Total: 0

Page 39

Problem 1: ? = $\frac{1}{24}$

Explanation: Divide both sides on 2nd balance in thirds so = $\frac{1}{6}$, so = $\frac{1}{3}$. Substitute $\frac{1}{3}$ for on 1st balance so + $\frac{1}{3} = \frac{1}{2}$. Remove $\frac{1}{3}$ from both sides so = $\frac{1}{6}$. Divide both sides in fourths so = $\frac{1}{24}$.

Problem 2: ? = 4,500

Explanation: Double both sides on 1st balance so 20,000 = + 2,000. Remove 2,000 from both sides so 18,000 = . Substitute 18,000 for on 2nd balance so 18,000 = . Divide both sides in twelfths so = 1,500. = 1,500 x 3 = 4,500.